"Thank you for writing this book; it changed my life."
~ *Marie*

"God has used your courage to be open about this subject to bring His hand of healing into my life and that of my sister, my husband and hopefully my mother. I, like so many survivors, felt like I had dealt with that part of my life. I see now that I really hadn't and it was still negatively affecting my life. Thanks for helping me look at this again so that God could provide the further healing I needed." ~ *Kimberly*

"What a joy to read a book that not only gives real, Biblical advice on how to overcome the pain that sexual abuse causes in our lives and marriages, but one that is clearly filled with the Holy Spirit. The gentle, loving hand of the Father could be felt through-out. Thank you!" ~ *Kellie*

"Working on this book, from concept to finished product, has not only helped me to more fully understand my own struggles and healing process, but to recognize how to use my experiences to help others." ~ *Kathryn*

"I really loved how you related the stories to the bleeding woman in the Bible, because isn't that what we are all doing on the inside? We are bleeding and need God's healing from all the horror that brought us to this point in the first place." ~ *CherylL*

"With sensitivity and compassion Sue Cameron encourages women who have been sexually abused to seek the healing only Jesus can give. You won't find pat answers or easy answers, but you will find God's answer as Sue shows you how to apply the truth of Scripture to your life. This book will change your life! It is must reading for anyone who has been abused and for their spouse and friends who want to help but often don't know how." ~ Marlene

# Hope, Healing, and Help

## for Survivors of Sexual Abuse

### A Faith-based Journey to Healing

Sue Cameron

ISBN: 978-0985071004

**GSC Publishing**
El Paso, TX 79912
GrammySue.com

For You ~ My Friend

For my childhood friend who suffered so much.
How I wish I had spoken up for you then.
I am speaking out now.
I admire your strength and courage
and will always love you.

# Special Thanks!

I give thanks to the Lord for ~ my husband, Craig, and his constant support, love, and patience with me as I've sought healing from my own sexual abuse and endeavored to follow God's call to write about it.

My faithful friend, Marlene Bagnull, who has worked alongside me, believed in me, and not allowed me to give up or give in. Her encouragement has indeed given me courage.

The precious group of survivors who met with me to read, review, and comment on this manuscript, sharing their own stories, wisdom, and insight to help this book be authentic. They stuck with me for nearly two years, even though I told them at our first meeting, "It should only take about six weeks."

Katie Gray, my faithful reader and researcher, who helped do the behind-the-scenes work of finding the facts and editing my words.

My son, Eric, for the cover design and formatting.

Those who prayed.

Thank you to each of you!
You are precious to me, and I know that
we are partners in this work.
May the Lord be honored through these pages.

# Contents

# Introduction

Dear Reader,

We're survivors, you and I—connected because we've each experienced sexual abuse. And we're not alone. One in three women and one in five to one in seven men are also invisibly joined to us.[1] The details of our stories are as varied as we are, and none of us are exactly the same in how we've faced life afterward.

Whatever your response, it is valid. You're the only one who can determine the effects of your experience. But that doesn't mean you must face the aftermath alone. We want to come alongside you and say that the journey to healing is worth every difficult step. Dealing with a painful past requires great courage. We believe you are strong enough to begin the process.

In these pages you'll read about other survivors who acknowledge that sexual abuse still casts its fearful shadow on our lives. It threatens even our most precious earthly relationships. Should we simply allow our painful past to continue to torment us by robbing us of the intimacy God intends for us to enjoy? Is it fair for our innocent mate to also suffer from the injuries perpetrated against us because our wounds are still open and bleeding?

It's time for the pain to end so we can go on to live the rest of our lives without regret about how we've chosen to deal with our abuse. We desire strong and lasting relationships, whatever the cost. We refuse to be defined by what happened to us. We want our lives back—whole and healed.

While this book is written primarily for married women, its pages are intended to lead all readers toward the Lord who heals. If you have doubts about a loving God because of the trauma you experienced, your feelings are valid. It's okay to have issues related to God. But before you decide that He is untrustworthy, please give Him the chance to heal your pain as He is doing for us.

Healing is a process. There are biblical principles that have helped other survivors to find freedom from the effects of their sexual trauma and to embrace a new future. It is the Lord's good intention for each of us to enjoy a healthy, satisfying, intimate relationship with our life partner. It's the reason we seek healing from the effects of our sexual abuse.

With the exception of my own story, the stories are composites of true accounts that have been put into story form. Like ointment on a raw wound, we pray that these stories will help you identify and address the source of your pain and find relief for your weary soul.

I am indebted to a group of survivors who met together to read, analyze, and comment on these pages. They've shared their insights and experiences to make this book useful and encouraging to you.

When the words *us, our,* or *we* are used, it refers to this courageous group of women. We invite you to join hands with us as we take this journey to healing.

*Chapter 1*

# Go Away—I'm Fine!

## *Teri's Story*

Pounding on my sister's apartment door, I yelled, "Teri, open up. I know you're in there."

"Go away."

"I'm not going anywhere."

"Just leave me alone."

"Just leave you? That's what you want?"

"Yeah, so?"

A part of me wanted to turn away, to go back down the stairs and out into the fresh air. *I'm getting so tired of trying to help her.* But another part of me completely understood. We'd grown up together. We'd shared the same parents, the same kinds of pain. *She's my baby sister. I can't just abandon her.*

"So?" I shouted at the closed door with the peeling paint. "I love you and you matter to me."

I waited. *Lord, please let her answer.*

Several moments passed before Teri opened the door a crack and peeked out. Her puffy red eyes were filled with deep sadness.

Wedging my snow boot into the opening and heaving my shoulder against the door, I stepped inside. She shrunk back with a look of terror.

Locking the door, I said, "It's okay. No one can get in."

The heat felt stifling compared to the winter air outside. I shed my scarf, coat, and gloves and tried to adjust to the darkness. Her place was like a cave with the curtains drawn. The air was stale.

Straining to see, I followed her, stepping around piles of empty boxes, dirty clothes, and litter as I made my way to the dilapidated sofa. Before sitting next to her, I turned down the TV and pushed aside discarded food containers.

I took her hand. "Can we talk?"

"About what?"

"There's something really important I want to tell you."

She nodded but kept staring at her lap.

Moving clumps of matted hair gently away from her eyes, I said, "Look at me—please pay attention, okay?"

Our eyes met. I almost looked away. It hurt to see the depth of sorrow reflected there. *It's gotten worse. Time doesn't heal all wounds.*

"There's a group at church that I've been attending for a few months, and it's helping. I'm better."

She yanked her hand out of mine. "I don't want to hear about it." She turned away.

Trying to keep my voice calm, I said, "Really, Teri, I'm starting to experience life in a new way. It's like everything was dull and gray and now—now it's in color. God's changing things for me."

"What's Jim think?"

"He didn't like the idea at first. Thought they were a bunch of religious fanatics. But then, considering how awful our marriage was, he said it couldn't hurt."

"Was?"

"Yeah, it's even helping our marriage."

I had her attention. "I don't have as many nightmares," I said. "And my headaches have gone away. The Lord is healing me."

"Your headaches are gone?"

"It's been nearly two months since I had one."

We sat in silence until she said, "Steve called yesterday."

"Really?" A glance at her left hand confirmed that she still wore her wedding ring. "How long has it been since you heard from him?"

"Since summer."

"How did he sound?"

"Good . . . really good." Her mouth twisted and she blinked back tears. "I think he's doing better without me."

I pulled a tissue from my purse and laid it on the sofa next to my sister. "It's obvious you miss him."

She nodded, picked up the tissue, and blew her nose.

"Do it for Steve," I said gently. "It matters." I handed her another tissue. "Jim even held my hand when we were at the grocery store the other day."

"Yeah?"

"Now that I'm dealing with my problems, it's like I can think of ways to—I don't know—to take better care of him."

Her mouth compressed into a sort of pucker. She always did that when she was thinking.

"It's not as scary as you think," I said.

"Wanna bet?"

"Okay. You probably feel like leaving this apartment will destroy you, but it won't. It's hard, but it's worth it."

She looked at me as if she doubted me.

"It's true," I said. "I can get on a bus now and not feel afraid of all those strangers. It's so freeing."

She glared at me. "Well, I'm so thrilled for you."

I felt like she'd stabbed me. My first instinct was to lash out at her or maybe to simply get up and leave. Instead, I took a deep breath. "You can't scare me away. You always get mean when you're afraid and don't want to listen."

"Why should I listen?"

"Because, I'm telling you the truth. The Lord wants to make you whole, to give you a good life, to take away your pain. He can do it."

She looked at me but remained silent.

I kept on. *Lord, help me to persuade her.* "I'm learning that the way I think affects my feelings and that what happened isn't my fault. Listen," I forced her to look at me, "we are not to blame. Isn't that wonderful news?"

Teri didn't look convinced.

"I want you to get better, too. All you need to do right now is come with me to the meetings—please."

"No. I don't want to go. You-know-who will find out and hate me."

"They're the ones who hurt you—who hurt us."

"I'll make them mad. They're mad at you."

"I'm sorry about the way they feel. But—" I swallowed my panic. "I'm responsible for my life and my choices now." I took a deep breath. "Maybe they'll want to be free too, when they see how I've changed." *I hope so.*

"I don't have anyone else. I'm all alone."

"No." I placed my hand on hers. "You have me and Jesus, both of us. We'll be with you. I know you're sick of living like this. You must want to get better."

She nodded.

"What happened back then is ruining your life now."

"I don't like hurting this much."

I stood. "Come on. Let's go right now."

"I can't. I don't want to."

"I'll stay right with you."

"They'll ask me questions."

"You can just listen. You talk only when you're ready."

"I can't talk about those things."

"That's exactly how I felt. But when I finally started to talk about all that horrible stuff, it was like emptying an over-flowing trash can."

Pausing, I waited for a reaction. When she didn't respond, I said, "It took so much energy trying to keep the lid on my stuff that I didn't have strength for anything else. It wore me out. You know what I'm talking about."

"Opening up is like making room in your soul. It's dumping the garbage so it doesn't fester inside anymore. No more stink. It made me feel free and light. Now I can think of other things—like the flowers I saw in Mrs. Gordon's front window this morning."

A glimmer of light appeared in her pale blue eyes. "I used to like flowers."

I took her hands and helped her to her feet. "I know. Remember those roses in our yard when we were little girls? They were kinda purple . . ."

"I loved the way they smelled."

"And you picked some once to give to Mother."

She stiffened. I wished I could have taken back the words. *You were beaten and locked in a closet for that act of kindness.* "I'm sorry, Teri. I didn't mean to remind you of—"

She seemed to withdraw into a dark cavern as she sat down on the couch pulling her feet under her.

I knelt before her. "See, this just proves how wounded you are. I understand. If you'll come for help, then when you remember the bad things, you'll be able to go on without them making you feel so worthless."

Rubbing the back of her hands, I said, "You don't have to stay like this."

"I'm fine," she snapped.

"But it's obvious that you're still hurting."

"There's nothing wrong with me. Leave me alone."

"Please. You can get better, too." She started to retreat, to pull away. Her eyes dimmed.

"It's taking time, but things are changing for me." I saw it was too late and I couldn't stop my tears. *I've lost her to the dark place.*

I stood again and took her hand. "Please come with me. Please!"

My tears didn't touch her. My pleading failed.

Defeated, I finally left my sister sitting there, alone in her pain. I knew where she could get help, but I couldn't make her go there. *I'll try again, later.*

Leaving her apartment, I made my way down the stairs, out the door, and got on the waiting bus. And I wasn't afraid.

## Relating to the Story

- ❖ Do you relate to either of these women? If so, which one?

- ❖ Why might Teri refuse to go for help?

| Not ready | Frightened | Doesn't want to feel out of control |
|---|---|---|
| Afraid of change | Is comfortable as "the victim" | Feels unsafe without boundaries |
| Can't face her pain | Feels unworthy of a better life | Has decided to live with her pain |

- ❖ Do you feel any of the emotions listed above?

- ❖ Is it easy for you to admit when you're hurting and need help?

Very easy----------------------------------------------------Very hard

- ❖ Do you think Teri might get better if she went for help?

No-------------------------Not sure---------------------------Yes

❖ What might it take for Teri to be willing to go for help?

❖ Has anyone encouraged you to seek healing for the sexual abuse you experienced?

No one-----------------------------------------------------------------Yes

❖ Do you know of anyone else who has experienced healing from their past? If so, how does the fact that they are better make you feel?

| Hopeful | Jealous | Scared |
|---------|---------|--------|
| Pressured | Hesitant | Skeptical |

❖ Would you rather seek healing alone or with another trusted person?

Alone-----------------------------------------------With someone

❖ Rate where you are, at this moment, on the journey toward healing.

Open wounds-----------------------------------------------Healed

## Recognizing the Issues ~ See the Need

It's heartbreaking when those we love refuse to get help. As much as we want you to find healing, we know that you don't have to come along with us. If you are hesitating, unable to take the first step, we understand.

Maybe you will set this book aside for a time. That's okay. But it's our hope that you won't waste another day of your life in misery. The decision is yours. Just remember, you're not alone. We understand. We've been there.

If you think you're ready to go on toward healing, please allow us to take you by the hand and show you the way. The first step is to recognize the need. It's admitting and accepting thoughts like, "I'm hurting," "I'm still being affected by what happened," "I wish I could get over the past."

No one can force you to take this step. Even though you may not fully comprehend what the journey to healing will actually be like, you must be willing to take the risk and go forward. When you do this, you move away from your current suffering. It's like leaving a very dark place and inching toward a tiny glimmer of light.

One way to do this is to keep reading this book. We want you to. Read with an open heart and you will discover that the direction you are heading offers new life.

## Requesting God's Help

Here's a prayer before we take a close look at a Bible passage.

"Lord, thank You for caring about us and the details of our lives. Please give us open hearts and minds to hear Your voice. Teach us through Your Word. You are the only One who knows us inside out and understands all that we feel, all that we think, and all that concerns us. Please, Lord, show us how to listen to You. Help us to trust You in new and deeper ways. When we feel afraid, give us courage. Amen."

# Reflecting on Scripture

Chapter by chapter we'll focus on a woman who was healed by Jesus. Her story is recorded in Mark 5:25-34. We encourage you to read it slowly, several times, and to think carefully about its meaning. There will also be questions to consider if you want to go deeper.

Here is the whole passage so you can get a grasp of the entire account. There is supernatural power in the Bible. As we seek to understand its meaning, we begin to change in positive ways that impact every aspect of our lives, especially our close relationships. We pray that this will also be true for you.

## Mark 5:25-34

25 A woman in the crowd had suffered for twelve years with constant bleeding.

26 She had suffered a great deal from many doctors, and over the years she had spent everything she had to pay them, but she had gotten no better. In fact, she had gotten worse.

27 She had heard about Jesus, so she came up behind him through the crowd and touched his robe.

28 For she thought to herself, "If I can just touch his robe, I will be healed."

29 Immediately the bleeding stopped, and she could feel in her body that she had been healed of her terrible condition.

30 Jesus realized at once that healing power had gone out from him, so he turned around in the crowd and asked, "Who touched my robe?"

³¹ His disciples said to him, "Look at this crowd pressing around you. How can you ask, 'Who touched me?'"

³² But he kept on looking around to see who had done it.

³³ Then the frightened woman, trembling at the realization of what had happened to her, came and fell to her knees in front of him and told him what she had done.

³⁴ And he said to her, "Daughter, your faith has made you well. Go in peace. Your suffering is over."

## Responding to God's Word

The Bible records true accounts of real people. People the same as us. When we read about them, we often learn about ourselves. Slowly read the verse printed below and respond to the questions.

**Mark 5:25**

**A woman in the crowd had suffered for twelve years with constant bleeding.**

❖ This verse refers to a person of what gender?

❖ Where is this person?

❖ What two words describe her physical condition?

❖ How long had this been going on?

❖ What word describes her emotional state?

Here's a woman in a large crowd with a very personal problem. It's not likely that she talks publicly about her pain. The hurt she endures is hidden, private—a shameful secret. Her condition has isolated her from others. Perhaps only those who know her intimately are aware that she lives with constant pain and bleeding.

But maybe no one knows. Day after day, year after year, she may have suffered alone in silence. She may feel overlooked, unimportant, and worthless amidst a multitude of people. No doubt she is weary. Worn down and worn out— weak. One thing is certain; she knows she is suffering and admits, at least to herself, that she is in pain.

❖ Can you relate to this description?

Not at all---------------------------------------------------Totally

❖ Do any of the words below feel familiar to you?

| Frightened | Wounded | Weary |
|---|---|---|
| Shameful | Alone | Overlooked |
| Worthless | Isolated | Suffering |

❖ If this woman were your best friend, what would you advise her to do?

❖ Rate the amount of suffering or pain you have at this
point in your life.

None-------------------------------------------------------Constant

One thing is clear about the woman described in this
passage; she is completely aware that she is suffering and that
pain has been a part of her life for years. Her story offers us an
example of a courageous woman who has taken the first step
toward healing by admitting she has a need. If she hadn't, we
would not be reading her story today.

This woman isn't in denial. She isn't saying, "Nothing's
wrong," "I'm fine," or "I'll just put up with it." She knows what
it's like to live with the constant, uncomfortable reminder
that something is not right.

We'll consider more of this woman's story as we go. Let's
try to become very attentive to the ways God may be speaking
personally to us through this passage. He may use nature,
conversations, reading material, everyday occurrences, or the
media.

By allowing these thoughts and concepts to roll around in
our hearts and minds we will gain spiritual insight. Let's ask
the Lord to give us wisdom and expect Him to reveal truth to
us. He wants to. He is faithful to communicate to us in ways
we can understand. He will speak to each of us in a personal
way; our part is to learn to listen.

## Releasing It All to the Lord

"Lord, God of Mercy, thank You for totally understanding
each of us. You know our fears, insecurities, and pain. Thank
You that when You call us, Your voice is soft and kind and
You truly adore us.

"Please help us to want to be healed. Give us courage to come to You and to let You take us step-by-step to wholeness. You came to bind up the brokenhearted and to destroy the works of the devil.

"The evil acts perpetrated against us have broken our hearts. Please bring us healing! Please make us whole. Let us enjoy life and our family. Strengthen our relationships. Teach us how to maintain healthy, satisfying, long-term intimacy. Make all things new. We can't do any of this alone, but with You all things are possible. Amen."

*Chapter* **2**

# Mommy, Is It Okay to Lie?
## *Mary Lynn's Story*

I sat on the floral sofa in my grandparent's trailer, waiting for my daddy to come and pick me up for the day. I touched the bows on my black patent leather shoes. I felt so pretty in my favorite pink dress. "When's he coming?" I asked.

My mother took a puff of her cigarette and glared at me. "He should be here soon."

A short time later, I heard the sound of car tires in the gravel. "He's here!" Before long, I sat beside him on the bench seat of his 1955 Chevy as we headed for the county fair. "Daddy, I want to go on the merry-go-round."

His smile made me feel warm and safe. "Of course, Little Bug. We can go on all the rides you want. This is your day."

"Can I have cotton candy?"

"Yes." He smiled. "And ice cream, too, if you want."

I leaned my head against him. His arm felt strong. "I miss you, Daddy."

He glanced down at me.

"Why do you look so sad, Daddy?"

"Because I miss you, too. You're my Little Bug."

I laughed like I always did when he called me that.

"Anyway," he said, "we're together today, and I promise that we'll have many other days just like this one."

"Will I see you even though you and Mommy got a divorce?"

"Yes. I promise you that."

It was a sunny California day. We drove through groves of orange trees and by roadside stands. "Can we stop?" I asked.

Daddy and I ate oranges at a picnic table in the shade.

He wiped my mouth with a napkin. "Hey, Little Bug, I have a question."

"What?"

"Do you like Dan—Mommy's new boyfriend?"

I shrugged. "I don't know."

"Since Mommy's going to marry him, I want to know if you like him. He'll be your stepfather."

"Will he have to live with us?"

"Yes."

A sour taste rose in my throat. "I want to live with you, Daddy."

He placed his big hand over mine. "I'm sorry that won't work. You need to stay with your mommy."

"Can we go now?" I got up and ran to the car. Daddy followed and helped me in.

We drove on. "When will we be there?" I asked.

"It's about half an hour more." Then, Daddy said, "Mary Lynn, I really want you to tell me what you think of Dan, okay?"

I nodded.

"Do you like him?"

"Not really."

He looked surprised. "Why?"

I stared out my window, watching as we drove past telephone poles in straight lines.

"Little Bug," Daddy said, "why don't you like Dan?"

I didn't answer.

"Did you hear me?"

I nodded.

"Well?"

"Are we almost there?"

"Not long now." Daddy drummed his thumbs on the steering wheel. "Mary Lynn, do you understand that I want you to answer my question?"

I nodded.

"It's okay if you don't like Dan. But can you please tell me why?"

"Because he makes me touch him," I mumbled.

"What?" Daddy shouted. "Where?"

Daddy's voice sounded angry; he looked mean. I felt afraid to answer.

His voice got quieter. "Where does Dan make you touch him? Answer me, please."

I started to cry as I pointed to my daddy's pants zipper.

Suddenly, Daddy pulled the car off the road and slammed on the brakes. His face turned red. This time he didn't shout, but he still sounded mad—really mad. His hands squeezed the steering wheel. "Dan makes you touch him, here?" He pointed. "Really?"

I nodded and cried harder. "Daddy, am I in trouble?"

"No." His voice sounded stern. The car tires squealed as Daddy pulled out onto the road.

"Daddy, where are we going?"

He stomped on the gas. "We're turning around. Going back."

"No. Daddy, please! What about the fair?"

He didn't answer me as we sped back to my grandparent's trailer. I knew then that I had done something terribly wrong.

Things got even worse at the trailer. People yelled. My grandpa stomped; my grandma cried. They sent me to the small bedroom in the back of the trailer that I shared with my mother. I got up on the bed and crawled under the covers, pulling them over my head so I could suck my thumb without anyone seeing.

Everyone was yelling, and my stomach began to hurt. I cried because I had done something to make my daddy and everyone else mad. And I had ruined my fun day at the fair with Daddy.

After a while, my mother came into the room. I pulled out my thumb and sat up.

"Get up," she said. "You have to take a bath."

"But I want to go to the fair with Daddy."

"You're not going. I'll start the water. Hurry up."

I took off my shiny shoes and slipped out of my fancy pink dress. I climbed in the tub and my mother rubbed a wash-cloth on my back while I sat in the warm water.

"Mary Lynn," she said, "do you want to make a really nice man go to jail?"

I looked up at her. "No."

"Well, Dan will have to go to jail because of what you said. Jail is an awful place. He'll go there and it will be your fault. That will ruin our lives."

I wiggled my toes under the water. "Why?"

"Because I'm going to marry him so we can all be very happy."

I swallowed.

"You want us to be happy don't you?"

I nodded.

"You will make Dan go to jail by saying those things about him."

"I don't want him to go to jail."

"Well, then, all you have to do is go out and tell your grandparents and your father that you were lying."

"But I didn't lie."

"It's up to you. You can decide. You said you want us all to be happy, right?"

"Yes."

"And I bet you'd love it if we had a beautiful house and all kinds of nice things. Dan has lots of money. He said he'd get us a house with a swimming pool."

"He did?"

"Yes. I told you he was nice. But if you don't say that it was just a made-up story, we'll have to stay here and live in this old trailer with your grandparents. Is that what you want?"

"No."

"Me neither. I want a nice house and I want to be happy."

"Mommy, is it okay to lie?"

She lifted me out of the tub to dry me off. "All I want you to do is to go out there and tell them that what you said about Dan wasn't real. That's all. Say that he never made you touch him and that he's a nice man." She pulled a nightgown over my head. "They all know you love to make up stories. So, just tell them that what you said wasn't really true; say it was just a pretend story."

I blinked at my mother. I understood what she wanted me to do. But I didn't understand why everyone was so mad. *What did I do wrong?* I knew I had done something terrible. That's why I wasn't allowed to ride the merry-go-round or spend the day with my daddy. Everything was my fault. My grandparents yelled and my daddy was mad because of me. And it was my job to make sure my mother and I had a good life and a big house and lots of nice things. All I had to do was to say that I was lying about Dan and everything would be perfect.

## Relating to the Story

❖ Do you agree with Mary Lynn that everything that happened was her fault?

Not at all------------------------------------------------------------Totally

❖ Have you ever felt, or do you currently feel that what happened to you was your fault?

Not my fault--------------Partially my fault---------------My fault

❖ Did any adult(s) in your life cause you to feel responsible to make them or the family happy?

No--------------------------Sometimes-------------------------Yes

❖ If you answered yes, who was that person or those people who made you feel responsible?

❖ Of those listed below, which ones are responsible for Mary Lynn's sexual abuse?

| The boyfriend | Mother | Father | Grandparents |
|---|---|---|---|

❖ Who are the people responsible for your sexual trauma?

❖ Have you ever released yourself from any and all responsibility for the actions forced on you?

No--------------------------I'm trying--------------------------Yes

## Recognizing the Issues ~ Place the Blame

It's common for those who have experienced sexual abuse to blame themselves. They may think things like: "If only I had worn pajamas instead of a nightgown." "I shouldn't have gone fishing with him." "I'm the one who said I wanted to go on a picnic." "Why didn't I scream?"

To complicate matters, your abuser may have shifted blame to you by statements such as: "If only you weren't so pretty." "Your mother doesn't understand me like you do." "Never let me do that to you again." Or, "I can tell you like it too." These types of comments are used on purpose in an attempt to shift fault away from the perpetrator and to excuse their wrongdoing.

Such words can cause a survivor to assume false responsibility. One father told his children, "I'm doing this to you because my father did it to me." While he didn't cast direct blame on his children, he shifted the blame away from himself and failed to take responsibility for his own evil actions.

It's important to note that it is not our job as survivors to make sure our perpetrator(s) takes or admits the blame, feels remorse, or in other ways accepts responsibility. We have no control over other people, their choices, or their actions. We can only decide how we will think and respond to our own situations, our memories, and to the people in our lives.

Focusing our attention on those who hurt us only drains our energy and adds to our suffering. Concentrating on our own heart attitudes is the path to freedom.

Yet, releasing blame may be difficult for some survivors because it's finally admitting that we were powerless. Holding on to feelings of blame offers the false illusion that we had control. Letting it go can be frightening because it is acknowledging that we did not and do not have control over how others choose to treat us.

By embracing the fact that we are not to blame for the acts perpetrated against us, we gain power in knowing that we are in complete control of how we choose to respond and react to the things that happen.

Another factor that may lead to confusion, misplaced blame, or assuming false guilt is remembering any times when our bodies seemed to betray us by responding to some types of sexual stimulation.

This doesn't mean that we asked for the abuse, wanted it to happen, or that we are responsible. Such responses do not validate the experience as good.

Some survivors live under a great burden of shame because, over time, they grew to derive some physical pleasure from the abusive encounters.

Our bodies are designed to respond sexually even when the context is unhealthy. If this happened to you, the chances are good that your perpetrator seized on that fact to falsely accuse you in some way. But experiencing a natural physical reaction does not make you responsible for the abuse. You are *not* to blame.

Identifying who is *actually* responsible for the abuse we experienced is vitally important. We must place the blame on them. Please understand that while our minds may automatically think of the person or people who acted against us, our hearts and emotions may still accept some degree of fault.

Hidden thoughts such as: "If I wasn't so bad, it wouldn't have happened," "I deserved it because _____," or "If only I had _____," can be clues as to who we actually believe is responsible for our sexual abuse.

It may be that you secretly think you're at least partially at fault. To accept thoughts such as these without question is the same as saying they are true. This type of thinking has a negative effect because such thoughts are lies. In order to heal, it's necessary to confront these lies. But first, each one must be identified. This isn't automatic. It takes prayer, effort, and concentration.

Make it your goal to uncover your own true feelings about your experience—not what you think you should feel or believe, but what you actually do think and believe. This is an essential component of healing.

Each of us must determine if we are living our lives today based on truth about our abuse or on lies that we have unwittingly accepted as truth. When we allow feelings of guilt or shame associated with past abuse to go unchallenged, we are choosing to accept them as true. It's the same as believing a lie. Since lies are not true, they cannot support healthy living.

Lies are not solid; they are like Jell-O®. If we try to build our lives on what is false, our existence will feel shaky and unstable instead of secure and safe. We must have truth as the foundation of our lives and our relationships, especially our marital relationship. Falsehood is no basis for intimacy.

Until you truly believe and fully accept the truth that you are not at fault for the sexual abuse you experienced, you will not move on toward healing. We each must place the blame where it belongs—on the person or people who used our bodies for selfish gratification.

If you're reading this book, I believe it is in part because you care about your close relationships. If you're married, you love your husband and you want to experience the good, God-ordained side of intimacy.

You long to be whole. So, take some time, right now, to determine your true feelings/beliefs about the abuse you've survived. Start with prayer. (There's one printed below if you want to use it.) Ask the Lord to show you the truth about how you feel. It may be helpful to write your impressions in a journal or notebook.

## Requesting God's Help

"Lord, thank You that You know all things. You know what we think, feel, and believe. Please show each one of us what it is we believe about the abuse we've experienced. Help us to see if we have or have not put the blame where it belongs. Amen."

## *Reflecting on Scripture*

The verse we studied last time is printed below. The following verse (in bold) is the one we'll be considering today. Read it slowly and thoughtfully and respond to the questions.

### Mark 5:25-26

25 A woman in the crowd had suffered for twelve years with constant bleeding.
26 **She had suffered a great deal from many doctors, and over the years she had spent everything she had to pay them, but she had gotten no better. In fact, she had gotten worse.**

❖ What words in this verse describe this woman's condition?

❖ Has she sought relief from her pain?

❖ Were there other people who added to her suffering?

❖ How long has she been hoping to be well?

❖ To what lengths has she gone to get better?

❖ What were the results?

Can you relate to this woman even though you live at a different time in history? She's a woman who knows that something isn't right, who knows she's not well, and who desperately wants to get better. So she begins to search. She goes to those people who are trained to help her—the ones who are supposed to make things better. They fail her, yet she goes back over and over hoping that things will improve. They don't.

Maybe you know someone like this woman. Someone who has tried everything to get well. A determined modern-day woman who has read books, researched online, sought therapy, gone on special diets, used medication, engaged in counseling, paid for products, maybe even attended Bible studies and church and cried out to God. But the pain continues. It clings to her relentlessly, like a parasite, invading her body, soul, and spirit.

Nothing has worked. She's wasted time and money. There are no remedies left to try. She's out of resources. There's no money—no hope. Those near to her might have fled or been pushed aside. It's obvious that she's worse today than she was last year, or the year before, or the year before that. She's ready to give up. Maybe she's thinking *I'll just have to endure the pain and find a way to go on.*

❖ Can you relate to this description?

Not at all----------------------A little-----------------------Totally

❖ Do any of the words listed below seem familiar to you?

| Ready to give up | Tried everything | Still hurting |
|------------------|------------------|---------------|
| Nothing worked | Totally numb | Wasted time |
| Out of money | Secret pain | No hope |

| No help for me | Worn out | Lost relationships |
| --- | --- | --- |

This passage shows that there were other people who caused this woman additional suffering. How might she have felt about those people?

| Bitter | Angry | Resentful | Vengeful |
| --- | --- | --- | --- |
| Confused | Hurt | Unforgiving | Accusatory |

Consider how this woman's experiences might have affected her ability to:

| Be positive | Maintain relationships | Trust others | Be vulnerable |
| --- | --- | --- | --- |

Although we have no way of knowing the actual cause of this woman's constant bleeding, we do know that unexplained vaginal bleeding can be a result of sexual abuse.[2] Regardless of the reason for her hemorrhage, we know she is a woman who is suffering and who really wants to get better.

The places and people she's gone to for help have only brought her more pain. She's been disappointed every time. No one provided the relief she expected. She is broke. She has no resources left. It's unfair and unjust. She did her part but others failed her. They didn't come through.

Have you tried various ways to feel better that didn't work? As a result, maybe you have sought relief through alcohol or drugs or other addictive behaviors. Some seek emotional relief through controlling their own physical pain by cutting or unhealthy eating practices.

If any of these describe ways in which you have sought to relieve your suffering, think about how much you and the woman in this Bible passage are alike. She has tried everything, and she is still suffering. Her story holds truth for you and offers hope and healing.

## Responding to God's Word

When attempting to determine who is actually to blame for our sexual abuse, it's important to consider both those directly and indirectly responsible. There is the person or people who knowingly perpetrated the abuse in the first place. Also, there is anyone who knew of the abuse and allowed it to continue without intervening. Both bear responsibility for your suffering.

In contrast, there may also be people in your life who have unintentionally hurt you. The woman in our Bible passage must have felt this kind of pain. We assume that the doctors mentioned here did not intentionally add to her suffering; they simply didn't have the ability to make her pain go away. That fact must have caused her additional distress.

Over and over again she found the courage to seek out help only to be disappointed. She kept searching for an answer, but the Scripture says she only grew worse. Do you think she might have been feeling hopeless?

When our pain isn't addressed properly, it grows worse. There may be those in your life who have unintentionally added to your suffering because they couldn't ease your pain. That has made things worse for you. You looked to them, reached out to them, exposed your heart to them, and it didn't do any good. They were not able to offer you any lasting help. This is an important distinction to make when determining who is to blame for your pain. Clearly it is those who willfully hurt you and not those who were simply unable to help you.

Perhaps you thought that your spouse would ease your suffering. You may have believed that his love could make the pain go away. When you chose him, you were secretly convinced that he could untangle the knots of suffering that grip you as a result of what you've experienced.

Or maybe someone else has disappointed you—a close friend, family member, pastor, or counselor. They have compounded your pain, but not intentionally. Not every person we've turned to has hurt us. Some have aided us on our journey toward healing. But they, in themselves, could not remove the pain or restore our hope.

That is because there isn't a person on earth who can meet our every need or fill our every desire. It's unfair and unrealistic to ask or expect another person to do so. When we are empty, there is no way a person, or more food, or new things can fill us up. We have a big gaping hole in our spirit that can only be filled by the Lord. This is true even for those who never experienced the trauma of sexual abuse. We were created with a God-shaped space in our spirit, that only He can fill.

Each one contributing to this book has personally discovered that no person has the power to make us whole and bind up our broken hearts. That healing began at the crossroad where we met Jesus.

As we continue to read this Bible passage, verse-by-verse, I hope you are learning to be attentive to the ways in which the Lord is revealing truth to you. Many find it helpful to keep a journal where they can pour out their heart and record random thoughts and impressions.

Private writing like this can be one avenue where you unload pain and make room for fresh truth. For some, it is a place where they hear God's voice and record what He is saying. Even writing out the Scripture verses, the ones we're considering or others, can aid us in grasping their deeper meaning. In the book of Daniel, chapter 2, verse 28, we read "there is a God in heaven who reveals secrets."

## Releasing It All to God

"Oh Lord God, You are the One who reveals secrets. Please speak to us. Take us gently down the path where we can hear and accept truth. Only You can uncover the reasons why we are in this painful condition. Please reveal them to us. Show us what we need to know to get better.

"You alone know how hard we've tried, how much we've hurt, and how desperately we want to be well. Do we have to go on living in pain? Is this what You want for us? You see our suffering; You know how long it's been going on. We are weary. We are broken. We are without hope. Hear our cry for help and come to our rescue. Amen."

*Chapter 3*

# Courageous Confession

## *Amissa's Story*

My hand trembled as I hung up the phone and slumped to the floor. For many years I'd wondered how the news of my father's death would affect me. Now I knew.

Even at age fifty-seven, the fact that my own father had sexually abused me overshadowed all other memories of him. I always imagined that news of his death would give me a tremendous sense of freedom. In reality, I felt numb. That's all—just numb.

As I sat there on the cold floor, I remembered many details of life as his daughter. One day that I'd never forget was when I brought the truth out in the open for the first time. I had driven my friend's yellow Chevy to church . . .

~ ~ ~ ~ ~

My racing heart went into overdrive when I pulled into the church parking lot. It was Thursday afternoon so there were plenty of open spaces. Parking was easy. Getting out of the car was not. *I can't chicken out again.* Taking several deep breaths didn't ease the furious apprehension that urged me to flee from this whole ordeal. *No. I'm going to do it this time.*

Pulling the hood of my wool coat low over my face shielded me from the howling winter wind and from anyone who might see me there and wonder why I wasn't in school.

The note I'd forged about having a dental appointment worked surprisingly well. I simply left campus in a borrowed car and drove the back roads to get to my church.

Now, the bitter cold propelled me toward the warmth of the church lobby while my instinct urged me to run in the other direction. *I can't do this! What if I throw up? Maybe Pastor Redd will think it's my fault or that I'm lying.*

For years, I'd wanted to tell someone but never had the courage. I'd debated for months before making the decision to talk to my pastor. Without a doubt, what I was about to do would cause a lot of turmoil.

My life, and the lives of those closest to me, would never be the same. In fact, my family might even blame, reject, or disown me. But keeping the secret wasn't healthy for any of us. It threatened to destroy me. I had to make it stop and felt sure I was doing the right thing. With my seventeenth birthday only days away, it had to be done now.

My father had been promising me an extra special birthday surprise since last summer. Each time he talked about it he became more excited and I became increasingly repulsed. I couldn't endure another one of his *surprises*, regardless of how much he claimed he loved me, no matter how many times he told me I was special, or how often he called me "his little lady."

My heart finally began to calm when I heard the warmth in Mrs. Pearson's voice as she welcomed me. "It's so nice to see you. I'm glad you're feeling better."

Heat crept up the back of my neck at the mention of the lie I told to get out of last week's appointment. "Oh, yeah. Thanks."

Her smile was kind. "Pastor Redd is expecting you. But before you go in, I just want to tell you how pleased I am that your father has agreed to be the chairman of the deacons this year. I know he'll do an excellent job."

I felt the color drain from my face. *Everyone loves him. They won't believe me.*

Mrs. Pearson looked concerned and took hold of my elbow. "Are you sure you're feeling better, Dear? You seemed flushed and now you're quite pale."

*I can't go through with this.* I managed a weak smile. "I'm okay. I just need to sit."

"Yes, of course you do. I shouldn't be blabbing on like this." She knocked on a wooden door with a large glass insert and leaned in to say, "Amissa's here."

Pastor Redd greeted me and motioned me into his office. I sank gratefully into an overstuffed armchair and draped my coat across my trembling knees. Although my family had attended this church all of my life, I'd never seen this office before.

I glanced around at the beautiful greenery overflowing from ceramic planters. What a stark contrast to my desolate life. Suddenly, I wanted to weep. Instead I said, "Nice place."

"Thank you. I hope you're comfortable."

I nodded.

Pastor Redd turned to close the door. Panic grabbed me until I realized I could see Mrs. Pearson through the glass window. She noticed me looking at her and gave a small wave. I responded with a casual smile. *I'm safe.* I felt my shoulders relax.

Pastor Redd sat behind his wooden desk. He smiled and said, "It surprised me to see your name on my schedule today, Amissa. What's on your mind?"

I swallowed. *How do I say it?*

He waited.

All I could do was stare at my hands. I began to sweat. *This was a bad idea. There's no way I can tell him.*

Pastor Redd stood and my stomach tightened. When I saw he was only going to the water cooler, I let out my breath. *Breathe, just breathe.*

Pastor Redd handed me a cup. "Thought you might like some water." His voice sounded patient.

I took the small paper cup. "Thanks."

Before he sat, he positioned a box of tissues to where I could reach them.

*Guess he thinks I'm going to cry. I won't though.* I took several small sips, wishing I could just leave. Finally, I plunged in. "I have a problem."

Concern creased his forehead. "Is this a problem at school?"

I lowered my eyes and shook my head.

"At home—then?"

I nodded. *Just guess, please. Don't make me say it.* "Yes, at home."

"With your parents?"

I swallowed. "My father."

"I see."

I glanced at him and quickly said, "It's been going on since I was a little girl." I looked down again but peeked up to see his reaction. He didn't seem shocked or like he thought I was lying. He just listened. *He cares.*

Pastor Redd leaned forward on his elbows. "What's been going on?"

Suddenly, my throat tightened. My father's whispers of, "It's our secret," "If you weren't so pretty," "You'll send me to prison if you ever tell anyone," filled me with frantic fear.

"Amissa." Pastor Redd's voice sounded soothing. "Why don't we pray to get things started?"

We bowed our heads. He prayed, "Thank You, Lord, that You know all things. You understand how Amissa is feeling right now. I'm asking You to give her courage and peace. Help her to know You are nearby and uphold her with Your love. Amen."

*Help me, Lord.* "Amen." I looked at the empty cup in my hands.

"Would you like more water?"

"Yes, please."

While he was getting my water, he said, "Revealing what's hidden holds a certain amount of terror even for those who are brave enough to try."

I took the cup he offered. "Thanks."

Pastor Redd settled back into his chair. "The Lord is light, isn't He? So, when we draw near to Him, He sheds his light everywhere, even into the darkest places."

I nodded again, still unable to put words to my pain.

"Amissa, bringing our problems into the open is the only way to find freedom. Don't be afraid." He paused. "You were saying you have a problem with your father."

"Yeah." I stared at my lap. "I know that everyone thinks my father is a godly man."

He gave a slight nod. "Can you tell me what's troubling you?"

"My father's not as good as he seems."

"Please, go on."

"He does things to me—makes me do things to him—that are not right. I hate it."

"I'm listening."

I squeezed my eyes tight and forced myself to keep talking. "My father—has—is— sexually abusing me. He wants to take me to a hotel next week for my birthday so we won't bother Mother."

Suddenly, my words had their own momentum, like a train surging down the track. I opened my eyes and nearly shouted, "I just can't do it anymore! What if I get pregnant? He won't admit anything. He'll even blame me and accuse me of sneaking around with boys. That's a laugh, since he refuses to let me date or even go out with my friends—even friends from church. But I'm nearly grown.

"Can't I have a life of my own? I want to get married someday. How can my father claim to be a Christian and do these awful things to me? And how can God allow me to suffer like this? Do I have to go on letting him do it, just because he's my father? Oh, how I hate him when he touches me."

My voice trailed off and I gulped. That's when I saw my pain reflected in my pastor's eyes.

The rushing train slowed. An inward silence like the light of dawn began to expand inside of me. Into that stillness a feeling—like raging water breaking through a dam—overtook me.

Quivering, I watched the first teardrop hit the back of my hand. I grabbed a tissue as a shudder in my heart leapt up to form a soft sob. Tears came all at once and sounds of grief and anguish—ugly utterances from deep within and from long ago when I was so little and so scared and so confused. I mourned for all the mistreatment and shame that defined my childhood. My insides churned, shifted, and resettled, only to heave again—over and over and over.

Pastor Redd allowed me to cry. When at last the reservoir of my sorrow had emptied, he said, "Amissa, you have shown great courage today." His voice was kind but firm. "Let me assure you that the Lord is stronger than anything we face. He has promised to never leave us."

Peace settled over me as he spoke. I grabbed a handful of tissues.

"The situation you've describe is very serious," he said. "So, with your permission, I'd like to ask Mrs. Pearson to join us as we continue to talk about this. She has experience with matters like this. Will that be acceptable?"

I shrugged. "Okay."

As my pastor rose to call Mrs. Pearson into the office, I felt a lightness I'd never ever known before. *Maybe this is how living in the truth feels.*

~ ~ ~ ~ ~

The memory faded. . . . I got up off the floor knowing that although telling my pastor was the hardest decision I had ever made, doing it had been life-changing. *Thank You, Lord, for helping me to tell.*

As I finished that simple prayer, I sensed the Lord giving me courage to make another hard decision. *I will go to my father's funeral and comfort my mother.*

I knew I wouldn't go alone. Jesus and my husband, children, and grandchildren would all be there beside me.

That thought filled me with gratefulness. *Thank You, Lord, for healing me and for giving me such a supportive family of my own.*

## Relating to the Story

+ Can you relate to this story? If so, why?

+ Do you think families that go to church might have the types of problems revealed in this story?

No way------------------Not sure----------------Without a doubt

+ Did the person/people who abused you go to church or not?

Yes-------------------------Don't know-------------------------No

+ If they claimed to have faith, has that fact affected your view of God?

Yes-------------------------Not sure-------------------------No

❖ During your painful experience did you go to God for comfort?

All of the time----------------Now and then----------------Never

❖ If you would label those who abused you as religious, which of these words might you use to describe them?

| Hypocrite | Manipulator | Conflicted |
| Confused | Fraud | Evil |

❖ Does everyone who attends church know God in a personal, life-changing way?

No----------------------------Not sure----------------------------Yes

❖ Have you ever told your story to another person you trusted?

Never--------------------------Tried----------------------------Yes

❖ If not, have you wanted to share your story?

Never----------------I've thought about it----------------Want to

❖ If you have told someone, what was the response or result?

❖ If you have not told your story, are any of these the reason?

| Too scared | Embarrassed | Don't want to |

## Recognizing the Issues ~ Distorted Faith

Tragically, it's much too common for sexual abuse to occur in families active in church. In their book, *Freeing Your Mind from Memories that Bind,* Fred and Florence Littauer write, "A majority of abusers are religious men who participate in church activities and leadership. Because they know their basic compulsion to family sexual abuse, they tend to build a good reputation in church and community as a cover."[3]

When church is used as a cover instead of as a place to truly seek, know, and worship God, it is a double betrayal. Not only are survivors wounded by the sinful acts perpetrated against them, their view of God is often damaged. In fact, the abuse they endured at the hands of those claiming to be followers of the Lord may be the very reason survivors reject the notion that a loving God even exists.

Sexual perversion can occur as a part of cultic worship or in the name of religious tradition. Satanic rituals and groups that promote polygamy, where young women are forced into *spiritual marriages* with much older men, are examples of this type of sexual abuse.

Religion can be used as a way to manipulate and control others. If you have survived this kind of abuse and are still reading this book that points to Jesus as the way to healing, you are very courageous.

Please understand that we are not promoting religion but a personal relationship with God through Jesus. As you read about how Jesus interacted with the bleeding woman you will get a clear picture of what God is really like. He is not hard to find; in fact, God is drawing near to you as you continue to seek healing. Here is a verse to encourage you: "If you look for me wholeheartedly, you will find me" (Jeremiah 29:13).

Whatever specific details surround our personal experience, it's wise to consider if our view of God has been affected by the fact that we were abused. Everything that happens to us affects us in some way. Some survivors may have drawn nearer to God as a source of strength and comfort; others may have pulled back from Him. As survivors, we may be unaware of how great an impact our past experience has on our lives.

This may be especially true in the area of belief and the way we interpret the world around us. We tend to form our core beliefs based on what we've known. For example, an individual raised in a religious family that appeared happy and loving from the outside but was actually abusive behind closed doors, could understandably end up with a distorted image of God and family relationships.

Have you ever seen a row of knitting come undone when a single strand of yarn is pulled? When the people who are supposed to care for us say one thing and do another, our view of a trustworthy God can unravel. If those who abused us claimed to know God, we may have reacted by turning away from anything having to do with the Lord. The experiences we've survived have colored our belief system in various ways. How has your view of God been impacted by your past?

Most survivors do not go on to become abusers. However, it has also been shown that an overwhelming majority of perpetrators did experience some form of sexual abuse themselves.[4] Those who did not find healing and recovery may go on to repeat the offense.

This is why we often see a pattern of sexual abuse passed down in families from generation to generation. But each survivor has the opportunity to stop the damaging cycle of sexual abuse and bring an end to this destructive family tendency. The fact that we were abused doesn't doom us to behave in the same way.

In addition to families, there are also a disturbing number of cases of sexual abuse occurring within organizations that are supposed to be wholesome—places like youth clubs, special interest groups, churches, and social networks, that we expect to be safe.

Authors Fred and Florence Littauer state, "Men and women who have faced significant feelings of rejection in their childhood and who have also been abused sexually have a strong tendency to devote themselves, at an early age, to a life of service to God or to mankind. It is one way they feel they can make up for their low sense of self-esteem" (172).[4]

This may explain why some people who have never found true healing from their own pain try to mask it through service to others. Such people may end up actually abusing those they had initially intended to help. Serving others cannot make up for feelings of worthlessness or mend a broken heart. Seeing the connection between low self-esteem and involvement in service-oriented programs helps to explain why perpetrators often show up in places like church or community/service organizations.

Another element of wounding can occur when a survivor reaches out for help and talks to a trusted professional such as a pastor, teacher, or youth worker. If her disclosure is dismissed or she is made to feel like she is at fault, the results can be devastating not only to the survivor but also to her view of God. She may have thoughts like, "If the Lord's representative won't take me seriously," or "If they think it's no big deal," or "If they don't care, then, why would God?"

If your abuser(s) claimed to be people of faith and as a result you don't want any part of God, we understand your feelings. Even more important is the fact that the Lord shares your pain. He knows why you feel the way you do and offers you all the time you need to work through your suffering. In fact, He wants to help you through that process. The Lord is waiting to show you how deeply and totally He loves you.

Right now this may not make any sense to you and you may not believe it's true. In the last chapter, when you were asked to make a mental list of those responsible for your pain, you may have included "God." After all, if He is all-powerful, He could have stopped the abuse—but He didn't. He's supposed to love you, so where in the world was He when you were being violated?

Honest questions like these may have led to severe doubts about God, His existence, and His love for you. You may have decided that since He wasn't there when you needed Him, you have no reason to be interested in Him now. This reaction is especially common if those who hurt you claimed to be people of faith.

This isn't a book of theology, and I am no theologian, but I do want to address such concerns in a general way. First, it's vitally important that we start by examining what God has to say on the topic. To put it simply, He hates and forbids all sexual abuse and sexual perversion. Just look at these Bible passages, one from the Old Testament and one from the New Testament.

### Leviticus 18:6

"You must never have sexual relations with a close relative, for I am the LORD."

If you want more information, I suggest you read the eighteenth chapter of the book of Leviticus in the Old Testament. It contains many more detailed verses recording God's instructions for sexual behavior and how He forbids intimate sexual contact except with one's spouse.

## Matthew 18:6

"These little ones believe in me. It would be best for the person who causes one of them to lose faith to be drowned in the sea with a large stone hung around his neck" (GOD'S WORD).[5]

Be sure of this, the Lord did not approve of the abuse you endured. He hates it. He forbids it. He is against it. He was not a willing participant. When you hurt, He hurt; when you suffered, so did He. Jesus is One who knows how it feels to be injured, betrayed, mocked, made sport of, falsely accused, tortured, rejected, ridiculed, beaten, and ignored.

Now, let's talk about sin and free will. Here is a basic explanation. God gives each person a free will. That means people can and do choose how to act. The Lord won't stop us from doing what we want, even when our behavior goes against His will or injures others. It grieves Him when we make foolish choices because those choices often bring pain to us and to others. The Lord loves us and wants the best for us. He knows the consequences that will result from each one of our wise or poor choices.

Every one of us has a sin nature which means it's natural for us to choose to go against God's ways. This is obvious from our earliest years when we first began to exhibit selfishness. No one has to teach a child to want her own way or to be self-centered or demanding. In fact, the opposite is true; we need to be trained to be less selfish, demanding, and willful.

It's also true that very young children are innocent in their sin. They don't yet have the understanding of what is good and what is bad, and they have not yet learned the difference between right and wrong. That is why when a young child is corrected, he can seem so heartbroken, as if to say, "I didn't know that was wrong."

Let's remember that when Jesus wanted a perfect example of what type of person would enter the kingdom of heaven, He brought a child forward and basically said, "Be childlike, just like this little one" (see Mark 10:15).

Those who abused us have a free will. They chose to misuse us for their own selfish gratification. God did not make them do so; in fact, He commands us to be kind and tenderhearted to one another. Perpetrators of sexual abuse reject God and His will as revealed in the Bible. They blatantly ignore God's standards and His design for human sexuality. But be sure of this—one day each one of us will have to answer to the Lord for all of our choices.

It's easier to think of the poor decisions of others than it is to analyze the merit of our own choices. We may not see that when we hold onto bitterness or anger we are making an ungodly choice that only adds to our suffering. So, the next time you think about how you've been wronged also consider how you've reacted to that offense.

Free will means more than having a choice about how to respond to what happens to us; it also enables us to decide what we will do with the claims of Jesus. We can accept Him or reject Him. He said He came to earth to show us what God is like, to take away our sins, and to give eternal life to all who believe in Him. We choose if we believe Him or not.

If you believe that the Lord is uncaring, distant, or not to be trusted, please consider if your view of God has been distorted by your experience. Then, read this account of how Jesus responded to our suffering sister to see a true picture of what God is like.

God isn't to blame for your abuse. He is for you. He is full of compassion. Jesus willingly healed those who came to Him, like the lady who had been bleeding for twelve years.

## Requesting God's Help

"Lord, only You understand the ways I've reacted to being sexually abused. It has colored my thinking about life and about You. Please help me to see You clearly and to know that You really truly do love me. Let me feel it, Lord. Wrap Your arms around me and let me know that You love me. I need You so much. And I come to You, just as I am. Amen."

## Reflecting on Scripture

Read the following passage, with this chapter's verse printed in bold, and respond to the questions. To help us in our study, the verse has been divided into three sections.

**Mark 5:25-27**

> <sup></sup>25 A woman in the crowd had suffered for twelve years with constant bleeding.
> 26 She had suffered a great deal from many doctors, and over the years she had spent everything she had to pay them, but she had gotten no better. In fact, she had gotten worse.
> **27 She had heard about Jesus, so she came up behind him through the crowd and touched his robe**.

Let's recap a bit. This woman has suffered for a long time. She's tried to get help, but nothing has worked. She feels worse all the time. Now she is sick and broke. This describes the situation she's in when she hears about Jesus.

## She had heard about Jesus

Don't you wonder what it is she's heard about Him? Did she overhear others? Or did someone come to her privately— a person who cared about her, a friend, or perhaps a sister who knew her desperate situation? "He touches blind eyes and gives sight" (see Mark 10:51-52). "The lame walk" (see Matthew 11:4-5). "I saw it for myself. The man reached out his shriveled hand, and in an instant it was made new. New, as if it had always been whole!" (see Matthew 12:13).

In whatever way it happened, the news reached her. She heard about Jesus, and what she heard must have been something that gave her fresh hope—that made her willing to try again.

It is our prayer that this little book has sparked a similar response in your heart. You have heard about Jesus from us. We are survivors of sexual abuse. When we came to Jesus, He began to heal us. Things are changing. We're getting better all the time; our lives are being restored. The pain isn't searing anymore, and our closest relationships are being transformed. We're on the path to wholeness. And our suffering no longer defines us.

❖ Are you at all like the woman in this Bible passage? Has hearing about how Jesus came to heal the brokenhearted caused a new hope to spring up in your heart?

No---------------------------A little---------------------------Yes!

## So she came up behind him through the crowd

Let's think for a moment about what it took for this woman to even get near to Jesus. Even if Jesus passed through the area where she lived, it still wouldn't have been that simple for her to go to Him.

She's been bleeding constantly for twelve years, so she is weak and most likely anemic. Just think about how hard it is to get out of bed when you don't feel well. I imagine that leaving her home took a great deal of effort. And then, there is the inconvenience and discomfort of bleeding. It's messy. There are no fancy rest stops with flush toilets, small trash cans situated within arm's reach, running water, soap, or handy machines hanging on the wall with necessary items.

Still, she had heard about Jesus, and what she heard has made her willing to make the effort, to take the risk, to leave her comfort zone, and to head into unknown territory. I bet that the closer she gets, the more determined she grows.

As a woman in those times, she's considered unclean while bleeding.[6] So, for a long time this woman has had to focus on avoiding physical contact with people altogether and crowds in particular. According to the customs of that day, if she touches anyone or they touch her, they would also become unclean. She has spent the last twelve years avoiding others. Loneliness was certainly a part of her suffering.

But on this day, the day she decides to go to where Jesus is, none of that matters. This woman wants more than anything to be well. She is tired of suffering and wants her life back. She is on a mission; she is looking for a miracle.

Even though she is weak and sick, she does the unthinkable. She actually pushes her way through the crowd. We'll see in the verses coming up that this isn't a small gathering of a few people. It's a massive throng. But even though she probably feels intimidated, she is determined to find healing. Maybe she figures it's her last chance. Whatever her thoughts, she makes the journey and then manages to push her way through the crowd to come up behind Jesus.

### And touched his robe

So, she does it. This weak yet determined woman manages to find Jesus. She pushes, wiggles, and slips her way through the crowd until she is there—right behind Him. Then, she reaches out and touches His robe. This is a deliberate, intentional act. It isn't an accidental bumping into Jesus in the hustle and bustle of the crowd. No, she reaches out, on purpose, to touch His robe. I don't know if she gingerly reached out to grip the tiniest bit of cloth with her fingertip, or if she flung out her open hand to grasp a fistful of fabric.

In the original language, the word translated "touch" means "to adhere to." That indicates that once she made contact with Jesus' robe, she clung to it in hope, in faith, at least for a moment.

Also of interest is the place where her touch intersected His robe. Luke's account of this same story says "the fringe of his robe" (Luke 8:44) which indicates the bottom of the hem or the fringe of his prayer shawl. So, did she actually get on her hands and knees and crawl to get close enough to touch the edge of His robe?

Perhaps she knew the promise in Malachi 4:2 that the Messiah would come with healing in his wings. The word for wings also refers to the corner or edge of a garment. If she knew and believed this, it means she may have deliberately grabbed hold of that part of His robe.

Or, picture this. What if she was behind Him, but not right up next to Him? Maybe He was there and she could just glimpse Him through the throng of people surrounding Him. She kept trying to get closer to Jesus, but others were pressing in so close that she couldn't reach Him. So, in desperation, she finally just thrust her arm through the masses of shoulders and bellies to grab hold of whatever part of His robe she could!

Another fact that adds to the difficulty of this woman being able to touch His robe is that Jesus was not standing still. He was in the middle of something else. An important man had begged Jesus to come to his house and heal his dying daughter.

Jesus was on the move. He had a mission. He was responding to a need. This is when our dear woman comes up behind Him. Maybe she didn't want to interrupt Him, or distract Him, or bother Him. He's moving; she's reaching. Maybe she is trying to touch Him before He gets away. In any case, we know that this woman is desperate and determined.

## Responding to God's Word

* ❖ Consider this woman and rate how badly she wants to be well.

Not at all----------------Somewhat-------------With all her heart

* ❖ What about you? Do you really want to be free of your suffering?

Not sure---------------------If it's easy-----------------Absolutely

Now, this is interesting. Our courageous, resolute woman doesn't march straight up to Jesus, point her finger in His face, and demand to be healed. She comes up behind Him. Why? She didn't have to approach Him that way; I assume she did this on purpose.

* ❖ Why might she have chosen to come up behind Jesus instead of in front of Him? Which of these might apply?

| Frightened | Embarrassed | Wanted a secret healing |
| --- | --- | --- |
| Felt unworthy | She was shy | Didn't want to be noticed |
| Feared rejection | She was humble | Fears being reprimanded |

What about you? You've heard that Jesus has healed us. Maybe you have fresh hope. Will you make the effort to leave your place of comfort and push past your fears and objections to come to Jesus? It's perfectly acceptable to come to Him just because you long to be well. He is the healer! He won't reject you. He knows your heart and He knows your need. It really is fine for you to come up behind Him, to stay unnoticed, like the woman did in this passage. The important thing is that you come.

❖ How much are you willing to do to end your suffering?

❖ What if the steps you must take to get well are not what you expected, planned on, or find easy or comfortable? Will you still take them?

I'm starting to feel like I know this woman. Even though she lived at the time of Christ, I feel connected to her, like she's a sister. She sets an example for us and shows us the way to move from suffering to wholeness.

In this verse, we see that she doesn't accept the role of victim. She doesn't stay in her place of suffering and self-pity, even though we know that she is weak and hurting.

Instead, she acts on what she hears about Jesus, the One who can heal her. She demonstrates great courage and faith to leave where she is and go to where He is.

Her faith challenges us to give up our excuses and take the action needed to seek healing. The point is we don't have to stay in a place of suffering; there is a way to healing. We only need to be willing to make the effort to go from where we are to the place where we will find the One who can heal.

## Releasing It All to the Lord

"Lord God, You alone know every day we have lived, our every thought and pain. You empathize with our suffering and want to see us whole again.

"Please make us willing to come to You. Please help us to leave our excuses and fears behind so we can see You clearly, even if we have misjudged You because of our experiences. Have mercy on us now and show us Your goodness.

"We are weak and wounded, Lord, and we seek Your touch. Help us to trust what we've heard—that You are the One who heals the brokenhearted and comforts those who mourn.

"You came to set us free, to forgive us, and to offer us a joyful, meaningful life. Please heal our relationships. We want to believe. Help our unbelief and please meet each one of us at our point of need. Amen."

*Chapter 4*

# Uninvited Intruder

## *Kelsey's Story*

Positioning the fan in front of my open bedroom window and directing it toward my bed, I switched it to high even though I knew it wouldn't be very effective against the stifling heat. Then, I decided that air was more important than blocking out the glare of the streetlight, so I only pulled my shade down half way.

Thoughts of my summer session midterms the next day had me worried. I reached for the generic bottle of antacid pills on my nightstand before letting my cotton robe slip to the floor. I climbed into bed and switched off the lamp next to my digital clock. *I hope I get some sleep tonight.*

Things don't always turn out the way you hope. If ever there was a night when I didn't sleep well, that became the night—the worst of my life.

I tossed restlessly, kicked off the sheet, and shifted my head on the pillow. And then, unexpectedly, like goose bumps rising on your skin without warning, I became aware of an uneasy feeling. *Is someone in my room?* I took a nervous breath while glancing toward my clock, but I couldn't see the normal glowing numerals. *How'd my clock get turned around? And why is it this dark?*

In that instant, I knew. The presence I sensed was a person —a man. He loomed huge at the end of my bed. I felt his penetrating glare and gasped. Hot terror shot through me, clutching me in its sweaty grip. It didn't release me until it was all over, and still to this day, the indentations of its fingers remain on my very soul.

Before I could think my next thought, before I could scream or leap to my feet or grab my cell phone, a fierce hand clutched my neck, pinning me to the bed.

"Shut up," he snarled. "If you make a sound, I swear, I'll cut you."

In the dimness, I saw the glint of metal from the knife he waved in front of my face. "Don't tell anyone," he hissed. "If you do—if you go to the police or tell anybody, I will come back and kill you. And it won't be quick and painless. Understand?"

I understood. Yet throughout the ordeal I heard his raspy voice repeat the warning over and over again. *What's going to happen to me? Will he kill me even if I stay perfectly still?*

In the dim light I concentrated on his mouth, the only part of his face visible under the ski mask. I wondered if I'd seen his mouth before, in an ordinary place on someone who looked normal. Maybe he'd smiled at me in a hallway at my college, or at the grocery store, movie theater, or even at my church. The thought sent a tremor straight through my heart. *Oh, Lord, please don't let it be someone I know.*

I focused again on his mouth with crooked, crowded teeth. *Ugly.* This is how I tried to occupy my mind while he carried out his attack. *Foul breath. Liquor? Did he always drink before he raped? Did it add to the thrill or numb his sensibilities?*

He held the knife in one hand and used his free hand to stuff something soft into my mouth. *I won't scream.* His breathing was labored, making me think he wasn't a young man. *Who are you? Are you a father? A grandfather? Are you someone I know?* There it was again, unbidden, the fear that he'd singled me out on purpose. *Does he know me? Has he seen me somewhere, or am I simply a nameless victim—a body without personhood?*

I realized that the only way I could ever identify him again was by the bulging scar just above his left hip bone, but to do so would mean I'd have to see him naked—again. I squeezed my eyes tight against the thought.

*Why didn't I close and lock my windows?* Even as I thought it, I realized that he had taken the precaution of shutting them and pulling my curtains. That's why his sweat dripped onto my quivering body. He used his knife to cut off my camisole and panties. I didn't move or resist. *Oh, Lord, let me live!*

As the back edge of the blade slid along my skin, I became numb. I felt detached, as if my body wasn't even mine. Like an observer, I viewed the whole assault from a safe distance. As he inflicted injury, I remained motionless except for the terrorized beating of my heart and the silent tears weaving their way down my once naive face. I told myself, *Let him have his way, and maybe he'll let me live. Don't aggravate him. Just keep breathing.*

Afterward, I realized that he'd stuffed a pair of my panties, from my dresser drawer, into my mouth. *How long had he been in my room? Had he watched me as I tried to sleep? Had he been stalking me? What other things of mine had he touched?*

By the time he left me, gagged, tied to the bed, naked, and trembling, there wasn't an inch he hadn't violated and abused. I knew that every single part of my life—all my memories, all my belongings, all my tomorrows—would be tainted by this betrayal. Just as his fluids were smeared over the inside and outside of my body, this act of violence would cover my entire life with the sticky film of defilement.

## Relating to the Story

❖ Have you or someone dear to you experienced violent sexual assault?

❖ Please choose the types of struggles you think this young woman might experience as a result of this trauma.

| Fear of men | Anger | Nightmares | Self-injury |
|---|---|---|---|
| Trust issues | Depression | Self-blame | Safety issues |
| Sexual dysfunction | Feeling powerless | Tainted view of God | Eating disorders |

## Recognizing the Issues ~ Powerful Thoughts

While reading this story, did you notice the way this young woman thought about her attacker and the assault she endured?

Our minds are constantly full of thoughts—good or bad, true or false. Some are old and have been with us since our earliest years. Others are new and enter our minds on a spiritual level or through the media, our experiences, or other people. If the young woman in this story were an actual person, she would have to live her life while trying to deal with an ongoing barrage of thoughts related to and resulting from being raped.

Previously, we talked about the importance of evaluating our own thoughts. Now, let's take a deeper look at this powerful concept. We'll start by suggesting practical ways to uncover our own core thoughts and beliefs. Once we identify what we think, we can determine if such thoughts are healthy or not.

This is vitally important because thoughts can actually usher us toward healing or hinder our attempts to move forward.

The concept of taking control of the way we think is critical to healing because some thoughts help us win victory over the pain of our past; while others link together to form chains of lies that can keep us bound in a prison of suffering.

Not every thought that enters our mind is true. We often form opinions based on our experiences instead of on eternal truth. Such opinions are really just our thoughts, either spoken or unspoken, that we have accepted. As long as we allow such thinking to go unchallenged, we will remain stuck in the aftermath of our abuse.

It's time for us to become a security guard for our own mind. No one else can, so it's up to each one of us. Let's start by asking the Lord for the wisdom to interrogate both the thoughts that have resulted from our upbringing as well as those that are constantly attempting to access our mind. "Lord, please help me to be aware of what I think and where the thoughts come from. Show me if they're true or not."

Learning to analyze our thoughts isn't as difficult as it sounds, but it takes practice. It's simply a matter of learning to pay attention to what is going on inside our marvelous minds.

Since our thoughts directly affect how we feel, our emotions/feelings can offer us clues about whether our thoughts are healthy or not. For example, say we're feeling fine and having a good day when suddenly, out of nowhere, we start to have unexplained negative emotions such as feelings of insecurity, fear, despair, anxiety, or doubt.

When that happens, it's time to take careful notice of the feeling and give it a name. "I'm feeling inadequate, or angry, or worthless." Then, reflect back to discover what made you start to feel that way. Was it something you heard or saw that caused you to think a certain thought? Or maybe it was a random accusation that came into your mind such as, "That was a stupid thing to do."

Isolating the feeling is the first step. It helps us to identify the thought that came before the emotion. Once we know the thought, we can figure out if it is a true or false thought. Don't blindly accept every thought that passes through your mind. Each one is powerful for good or bad.

Picture your mind as a garden plot filled with rich soil. This is the place where thoughts are planted, take root, and grow. False thoughts are like weeds. If they are not uprooted, they will grow rapidly and can even take over so that nothing of beauty can survive.

True thoughts are like excellent seeds that grow into healthy attitudes that bring strength and goodness into our lives. Tending the garden of our mind is our job. While it isn't an obvious occupation of healthy living, it is vitally important.

Think about the young woman in the story at the start of this chapter. If she simply allows the memory of her rape, the images of her attacker, and the resulting thoughts to rule her, what might the rest of her life look like?

In order to be a victorious survivor of such a horrendous ordeal, she will have to separate the truth about what happened from all the falsehoods. She might feel like men can't be trusted, but is it really true that all men are untrustworthy? No. Or, she might take the blame for the attack because she didn't close her windows, but is she to blame for the violence against her? Did she ask for it, want it, and cause it to happen? No. The fault rests on the perpetrator.

The young woman in this story will have to control her thoughts and not let her thoughts control her. So do we. In the beginning, God planted a garden. He put the man in the garden to take care of it.

In much the same way, it is our job to tend the garden of our minds to make sure that what we allow to take root and grow are only true and healthy thoughts. We decide which thoughts are allowed to stay and which ones we will pull up and toss out.

We said that the way we think affects how we feel. The next part of that statement is how we feel determines how we act. Our actions are another way to get to the root of what we really think. By examining the feelings that lead us to unhealthy behaviors, we can figure out our thoughts.

Just ask, "How do I feel when I start to crave anything in excess?" "Why am I acting this way, or why am I doing this thing that isn't good for me?"

Once we identify the action and determine the feeling that came before it, we can step back and figure out what thought or thoughts are underneath. Put another way, we can ask, "What is the seed that my feelings and actions are growing from?"

Let me illustrate this with a real-life example. In writing this book, I have to battle monstrous-sized thoughts that attack me constantly. Thoughts like, "It's too hard." "You're not smart enough." "Who are you to write a book?"

When I agree with these thoughts by simply accepting (believing) them to be true, I feel inadequate and think that I'm wasting my time.

I don't like those kinds of feelings, so I take action! I search for chocolate and eat it, do laundry or other household chores, or shop online. In fact, I'll do just about anything instead of write. But it isn't really the feeling that keeps me from doing the task; it's the thoughts behind the feeling.

The Bible tells us to "take captive every thought to make it obedient to Christ" (2 Corinthians 10:5 NIV). This means learning to evaluate the thoughts that dominate our lives to determine if they line up with the truth God has revealed in Scripture. The thoughts we accept as true form our core beliefs about life, about ourselves, and about our world.

## Requesting God's Help

"Lord, please help me to understand this concept. Teach me to take my thoughts captive to Your truth. Please make it clear to me if I harbor thoughts that are lies or thoughts that are hurting me or that displease You. I want to start to think in new ways. Please clear my mind, cleanse it, and let me start to think pure and good and true thoughts. Amen."

## Reflecting on Scripture

Let's begin our Bible reflection by rereading the passage up to this point. Please pay special attention to verse 27, which we studied last time, as well as to today's verse printed in bold.

### Mark 5:25-28

<sup></sup>25 A woman in the crowd had suffered for twelve years with constant bleeding.

26 She had suffered a great deal from many doctors, and over the years she had spent everything she had to pay them, but she had gotten no better. In fact, she had gotten worse.

27 She had heard about Jesus, so she came up behind him through the crowd and touched his robe.

28 **For she thought to herself, "If I can just touch his robe, I will be healed."**

The verse we're considering today gives us a glimpse into this woman's heart and mind. We see her motive and the reason why she dared to leave her comfort zone and make the effort to push through the crowd to touch Jesus' robe. We see the thought process that led her to take action.

This passage demonstrates the power of the way we think. This woman's thoughts led her to act in a certain way. We see that the thoughts she accepted as true are also what she believed.

This illustrates that her great faith wasn't subject to her feelings. I'm sure she was well aware of the flow of blood and still felt pain, but she demonstrates her faith by her actions.

We also see that her belief or thoughts about her situation motivated her to do something. In her case, her thoughts led her to seek healing.

Here is a very interesting point. The phrase, "she *thought* to herself," in Mark 5:28, reads "*saying* to herself" (emphasis added) in the Good News Translation. And in the parallel account of this story found in Matthew 9:21, the Contemporary English Version translates it "she had *said* to herself" (emphasis added).

Identifying our thoughts can be difficult. But these verses show us that what this woman thought to herself is also what she was saying to herself. So, the things we say to ourselves are the thoughts that we believe.

When trying to determine what you believe, it might be helpful to ask, "What do I keep saying to myself?" It is important to know what we are saying to ourselves about our experience, about our desire for healing, and about Jesus. Figuring out what we think can be pivotal to our healing.

As our dear woman prepared to go to Jesus, she may have said over and over to herself, "If I can just touch His clothing, I will be healed."

She might have repeated this in her mind as she walked out of her home and down the road, and when she pushed through the crushing throng to get close enough to touch Jesus.

Review verse 28 again to determine why this woman thought that touching Jesus' clothing would bring her healing. Something she heard convinced her that she needed to touch His robe. We speculated earlier about what kinds of things she might have heard. Now let's look at some additional verses which shed light on how some people sought and received healing from Jesus.

### Mark 3:10

He had healed many people that day, so all the sick people eagerly pushed forward to *touch* him (emphasis added).

### Matthew 14:35-36

The news of their arrival spread quickly throughout the whole area, and soon people were bringing all their sick to be healed. They begged him to let the sick *touch* at least the *fringe of his robe*, and all who *touched* him were healed (emphasis added).

### Luke 6:19

Everyone was trying to *touch* Jesus, because power was going out from him and healing them all (CEV, emphasis added).

These verses show us that news about the healing power of Jesus spread quickly even though there were none of our modern methods of communication. People in need flocked to Jesus and pressed in for the chance to simply touch His clothes.

This woman may have heard news like this: "Sick people from all around are being healed; all they have to do is touch His robe!"

Let's imagine what it might have been like if this woman personally knew some of these people. The deaf man she's known since childhood, who lives down the road, can now hear. The woman at the market who sells beautiful fabric, the one with the limp, isn't limping any longer. And when her own sister, born with eyes so terribly crossed, returned from her trip to Jesus, she could see the world in a new way.

We see in Scripture that throngs of needy people went to Jesus in hopes of finding help. Our woman was one of those people. She determined (thought) in her mind that all she needed to do was touch the tiniest bit of his robe—even the fringe—and she would be well.

She believed. She had faith, and her faith was coupled with action. She did not sit at home and simply hope she'd get better. She did not feel sorry for herself because she had suffered for such a long time and so many people had failed to help her.

We don't witness any bitterness over all the money and time she had wasted. No. She heard about Jesus and believed. Then, she acted on her faith by going to where she could find Jesus.

We see that today's Scripture clearly illustrates that the way we think is important when we read, "for she thought to herself." Our dear woman's thoughts motivated her positive action. This is confirmed when we read this verse in two additional translations.

Please take note of the bold and italicized words which show that the things she heard about Jesus altered her thinking, and her new thinking became the motive for her actions.

### Mark 5:27-28

After **hearing** about Jesus, she came up in the crowd behind Him and touched His cloak.
For she *thought*, "If I just touch His garments, I will get well" (NASB).

### Mark 5:27-28

When she **heard** about Jesus, she came up behind him in the crowd and touched his cloak, because she *thought*, "If I just touch his clothes, I will be healed" (NIV).

This woman's determination amazes me. She refused to allow her suffering to define her. When she heard about Jesus and how he made people well, hope sprung up in her heart. To allow this to happen she had to refuse to be angry or bitter over her past failed attempts to get well. She also needed to be willing to do her part and go to Jesus.

## Responding to God's Word

What about you? Has a new hope stirred in your soul as you've read about Jesus and how He has healed other survivors of sexual abuse? Hope is precious. Don't resist it or be afraid of being disappointed. Allow hope to shine a tiny light in your direction.

The way you think about Jesus may be starting to change. Perhaps you're beginning to examine some of your long held thoughts/beliefs. Don't let fear keep you from continuing on the path of discovery; hope will lead you to a better place.

Have you been able to identify some of the thought patterns that dominate your life? What happens when we determine that many of our thoughts are negative but true?

We don't want to uproot true thoughts, do we? But how are we supposed to deal with true thoughts that are like poisonous weeds? Do we just allow them to grow and take over? Stick with us as we address these questions. You will find freedom if you will continue to apply your heart to wisdom.

When evaluating our own thoughts, it's necessary to discern between true thoughts and half-truths. Half-truths are actually lies. Identifying them as false, even if there is some truth in them, can be a key component in determining our own deeply-held beliefs.

In order to understand this, let's return to our beloved woman whose story is teaching us so much. We'll use our imagination to speculate about other thoughts she may have had. For example, what if instead of having instant hope, she had some doubts when she heard about Jesus? We know what she ended up doing, but that doesn't mean her positive response was instantaneous or that she didn't struggle with thoughts such as the three listed here.

### 1. **"I've tried everything and nothing has worked.** *This won't work either."*

How might she have dealt with such a thought? The first part of this statement/thought (in bold) is true, but the second part (italics) is a false assumption based on past experience. This woman heard about Jesus. We assume she heard that He healed all types of sickness. Since we know what she decided, we can imagine her reaction to such a thought must have been something like this.

❖ "I've tried everything and nothing has worked, *but all who touch the robe of Jesus are healed. I'm going to go and touch the robe of Jesus."*

2. **"I'm weak and worn out.** *I can't handle making the trip; it's too much for me."*

This thought starts with a true statement but draws a false conclusion. When part of a thought is false, the thought is a lie and needs to be rejected. If our woman accepted this type of thought as totally true, she may not have ever gone to Jesus. How might she have dealt with such a thought? Not by ignoring it. She must have addressed it. I wonder if she thought something like:

❖ "I am weak and worn out, *but this is worth the effort. I'm going to do it."*

3. **"There will be a crowd, and I am not used to being with a lot of people.** *If they realize I'm unclean, they'll reject me."*

A thought such as this would have been difficult to overcome. Jewish law stated that our dear woman was unclean. That meant she avoided contact with others for at least twelve years.

I'm sure that the thought of a huge crowd intimidated her. In order to do what she did, she had to break Jewish law and risk ridicule. She was truly a woman of great courage, determination, and faith. She could not have based her decision to seek healing on what others might think. Neither can we. How might she have addressed her own negative thoughts about the crowds?

❖ "There will be a crowd, and I am not used to being with a lot of people. *This won't be easy, but I'm going to do it anyway. I want to see Jesus."*

We are responsible for what we choose to do about the pain we feel. No one can do it for us, and no one can keep us from pursuing healing. This woman believed what she heard about the compassion of Jesus and so she responded. She had to make a choice. We're thankful she made the right choice; her example of faith is inspiring.

When evaluating your own thinking patterns, remember that a thought that is only half true is one that needs to be uprooted. Negative, accusing, and discouraging thoughts do not come from God. They are weeds, and we must not allow them to remain in the garden of our mind.

In order to illustrate the concept of how thinking can motivate actions, let's imagine some of the types of thoughts such a woman might have been tempted to think and the possible results. We'll begin with what we know to be true from reading her story in Scripture.

- ❖ "I've been bleeding for twelve years."
- ❖ "I've tried everything. Nothing's worked."
- ❖ "I'm suffering with this illness."
- ❖ "No one has helped me. Others have added to my pain."
- ❖ "I've gotten worse."
- ❖ "I've spent all my money."

Each of these is a true thought that describes this woman and her condition. If we put these into the form of an equation, it might look like this:

**Bleeding + Twelve years + No help = Suffering.**

Now, let's consider what happens to each of these true thoughts when we add an all-important qualifier—"She heard about Jesus."

The things this woman heard about Jesus changed her perspective about the things that were true in her life. When she added what she heard about Jesus to the truths in her life, everything changed. She was given the opportunity to view her situation in light of the fact that Jesus heals.

When we add the truth that God heals the brokenhearted to our own situation, everything changes. Specifically, our thinking is changed. This woman's thinking may have been altered like this:

* ❖ "I've been bleeding for twelve years, *but all the sick who touch the robe of Jesus are made well.*"
* ❖ "I've tried everything. Nothing's worked, *but I haven't tried the power of God.*"
* ❖ "I'm suffering with this illness, *but I don't need to stay like this. Jesus heals.*"
* ❖ "No one has helped me. Others have added to my pain, *but Jesus is healing men, women, and children.*"
* ❖ "I've gotten worse, *but Jesus is restoring people and making them whole.*"
* ❖ "I've spent all my money, *but Jesus heals for free.*"

The statements listed above reflect a new equation of:

**Bleeding + Twelve years + Jesus = Hope.**

Do you see how adding Jesus to any situation changes everything? This little exercise in what the suffering woman might have thought gives an example of how adding the Lord to the true statements of life alters them completely. Yes, we have survived sexual abuse. We agree that no one should ever be subject to such trauma. It was, and is, horrible—but Jesus heals.

Let's consider one last "what if." What might have happened if the woman in this passage had chosen not to change her thinking? If she had believed or focused on half-truths such as those listed above, what would have been the most likely result?

Or, what if she simply accepted what was true about her life and refused to factor in the power of God? Do you think she might have just stayed home because she thought the effort would not be worth her trouble? If she had, she would have missed the opportunity to see for herself if what she heard about Jesus applied to her situation.

She would not have been healed; her life would have been defined by her of by her faith. Our dear woman would not have met Jesus, and that means that her story would not have been recorded for us to read. She impacted history by her choice.

## Releasing It All to the Lord

"Lord, we want to love You with all of our heart, soul, and mind. We want our thinking to line up with Your Word. Please cleanse our minds. Please help us to identify and uproot all things false. Please change the way we think and the way we view our situation, our lives, and ourselves. Renew our minds. Give us wisdom. Wrap our fractured lives up in Your restoring love and make us whole, healthy, and free. We need hope, and we need help. We need Your touch. Thank You for hearing us and for the way You will respond. Amen."

*Chapter 5*

# What's Wrong with Me?

## Gina's Story

I waited while Gina slowly locked her front door.

"Ready to go?" I asked.

She blew her nose and then stuffed the tissue in her pocket. "I guess."

"Come on. It'll be good for you to get out." I turned and started off at a fast pace. "We won't be long," I called over my shoulder, checking to be sure she was coming.

Gina fell in step beside me. "I don't know how you talked me into this."

"It's a beautiful morning to take a walk."

She grunted.

"I know you feel rotten and all, but exercise will make you feel better."

"I don't think anything will ever make me feel better."

"Take it from me—turning forty isn't life threatening."

"It sure feels like it," she whined. "What's wrong with me? My life's falling apart. I can't sleep. I'm depressed. I can't get my weight under control. I don't want Ted near me, and I ache all over." She paused. "Is it just old age?"

I stopped mid-stride. "Well, if you're old, what's that make me?"

She shrugged.

We walked on in silence until I heard her sniffle again. She reached into her sweatshirt pocket for another tissue.

*Better just say it.* Swallowing my apprehension, I plunged in. "Listen, Gina, I felt much the same way right around the time I turned forty."

"Really?"

I nodded.

"What did you do?"

"At first I read self-help books, went to doctors, and tried pills and natural supplements, but nothing really helped."

Gina slowed. The sad look on her face turned to despair.

I touched her shoulder. "I'm better now."

She stopped to look at me. "Yes." Her forehead creased. "What happened? What did you do?"

"I finally figured out what was really behind all my problems. It wasn't obvious at first, but I slowly realized that my past was still affecting me."

Gina's eyes darkened and she bit her lip.

I stepped closer and said gently, "I know it's not what you want to hear. But it was only when I began to deal with all the pain I'd stuffed inside that things started to change."

She took a step back, wrapping her arms tightly across her body. Her eyes grew wide and worry etched her face. "Oh, Mary, it can't be related to that. It happened so many years ago."

"But it still bothers you, doesn't it?"

Tears welled in her eyes. "Yes," she whispered, blinking.

I slowly reached out to touch her arm. "Gina?"

She looked up. Her eyes told me she was listening carefully.

"It's time that you talked to someone—a counselor or other professional. Or go to a support group, like that one at church. Tell them about being date raped."

"But I wanted to go out with him."

"He was five years older than you. He used you for his own pleasure."

"But I agreed to it—at first. I liked the attention and the kissing and touching."

I took her hand. "But you didn't want sex, did you?"

She shook her head. "I planned to save myself for my husband."

"He overpowered you; that's sexual assault. I know you say he was your boyfriend; but that didn't give him the right to force himself on you. He stole your virginity."

She suddenly looked fragile as if a slight wind could cause her to dissolve. "I was only fifteen." She paused and I felt the weight of her sorrow.

Her voice was barely a whisper. "You're the only one who knows what happened."

"It's time to talk to someone else." I squeezed her hand. "You can do this. You have to; it could change your life."

Her bottom lip quivered.

I didn't let go. "This won't be too much for you. You're stronger than you think. The Lord will help you and so will I."

## Relating to the Story

In this story, Mary suggests that Gina's health issues might be related to the sexual abuse she survived. The concept that her past abuse and present suffering might be linked had never occurred to Gina. This may also be a new thought for you. As individuals, we process fresh information uniquely. The idea that our past and present are closely linked may not surprise you at all. On the other hand, it might be a new revelation.

Revelations can be simple, almost insignificant, or they can be life-changing. I always prided myself in the fact that I could fall asleep anywhere at any time. Knowing that most people couldn't do this made me feel special or at least unique. I used to say that napping was my gift until I was diagnosed with a condition called Sleep Apnea. That's where a person's airway is blocked off during sleep. They stop breathing until they take in a big gulp of air, causing them to snore. People with this condition never really experience a deep state of sleep and are at a much higher risk for various health problems.

I began to wear a sleep mask at night, and let me tell you it isn't pretty. A long plastic hose connects the mask to a small machine that basically forces a continual flow of air into my lungs. Now, I sleep.

I never realized that getting up several times during the night to use the restroom, sleeping so easily during the day, and snoring loudly were all warning signs of a very serious medical condition. I simply accepted these as normal because they had always been a part of my life. In reality, I needed help to be healthy, but I just didn't know it.

A specially trained professional helped me make the connection between these symptoms and the diagnosis of Sleep Apnea. Learning the truth about my condition changed my life. Really!

The first night I slept without waking up was a wonderful, refreshing experience. I liked it so much that I still wear the ugly, uncomfortable mask every single night.

Making the connection between past abuse and current symptoms can be compared to discovering an undiagnosed medical condition. It can bring great relief to finally understand why we feel the way we do. In our story, Gina knew that things were not right in her life, but she couldn't figure out the cause for her unhappiness.

- ❖ Can you identify with her?
- ❖ Do you ever feel as if your life is out of control?
- ❖ Is it a struggle to manage your anxiety level or fears?
- ❖ What about feelings of helplessness or inexplicable aches and pains?

Here are some symptoms common to survivors of sexual abuse and often begin to show up around middle age. Review the list below and see if any apply to you.

| Depression | Compulsions | Chronic pain |
|---|---|---|
| Promiscuity | Asthma | Anger |
| Unexplained pain | Migraine headaches | Stomach ailments |
| Insomnia | Hopelessness | Flashbacks |
| Fear/anxiety | Memory gaps | Guilt/shame |
| Low self-esteem | Relationship issues | Self-destructiveness |
| Sexual dysfunction | Eating disorders | Victimization |

❖ If you identified with some of the symptoms listed above, have you ever considered that they may be related to being sexually abused?

Yes---------------------------------------------------------------No

Survivors may fail to link the negative symptoms they experience in their daily lives with the fact that they were sexually abused. But making the connection is a critical step in healing. Sexual abuse injures us in many ways—emotionally, mentally, relationally, and sometimes physically. We don't always comprehend the long-term influence or the exact ways we are affected by past trauma, but the Lord does. Let's ask Him to help us.

*Lord, please show me anything I need to know right now. Give me insight as I seek to be healed. Amen.*

## Recognizing the Issues ~ Make the Connection

Every person who has survived sexual abuse has been affected in some way. We must face this truth and admit it in order to deal with the implications. Only then can we put our sexual abuse behind us.

This might make perfect sense when reading it. You might even agree with the concept, but actually breaking through the shield of denial can be difficult.

After all, pretending makes us feel safe. If it never happened, or if we determine that our experience wasn't a big deal, we think we're safe from being hurt again. Then we can attempt to simply go on with life. It may seem to work for a while except at night when the nightmares come. Sooner or later we must face the fact that bringing the whole truth out into the open is essential for our healing.

Some of us have tried, for years, to deny this part of our lives by shoving it into a locked closet within our souls. Sometimes it is our own family who has forced us to keep the *secret* hidden. But hiding it doesn't work. Our abuse and its results don't magically evaporate because we want it to or because time passes.

For example, we may insist that we have gotten over the offense or forgiven our abuser, yet we may have panic attacks or get a migraine when we know we will see our perpetrator again. We have a present day physical reaction to something that may have happened many years ago. We may convince ourselves that we can keep memories hidden away and that they have no affect on us. The fact is that every experience of our past is still with us and has served to fashion us into the people we are today.

Now, let's consider some other reactions to sexual abuse. Sometimes, a survivor's mind will actually block out the indignities and pain of sexual abuse in order to cope with life.

In *Healing from Sexual Abuse*, a 1991 booklet published by IVP Books, author Kathleen writes, "Repression and denial are subconscious processes which . . . enable a victim to continue living until she can deal with her trauma" (5). This happens at a subconscious level, and it's not the same as determining to deny our past.

Such memories are called *suppressed* because they are not remembered, and they can remain hidden inside for a long time. However, once a person is strong enough to be able to deal with the truth of such trauma, memories may begin to resurface. This can be very troubling.

One reaction to such glimpses of a hidden past is to deny that the memories are real or even legitimate. This can happen when a survivor fears the possible result of allowing such memories to surface. *What I do remember is bad enough. I don't know if I can handle knowing more.*

Also, accepting these suppressed memories may also require that the survivor let go of a false illusion of a normal or happy childhood.

No wonder this is a difficult step. Be reassured that those who begin to remember past painful experiences won't do so until they are ready to face the truth. God is wise and tender. While being able to suppress memories may initially be the gift that helps a person to go on with a life that seems intolerable, keeping such memories repressed will only cause deeper pain.

You may not feel ready to face your monsters. The thought might be terrifying, and it may seem far safer to keep them locked away. It's normal to feel uncertain about bringing a hurtful past out into the open and to worry that the pain will be too great. But the truth is that trying to keep such secrets hidden is destructive.

Continuing to deny our past abuse requires an enormous amount of psychological energy. We exhaust ourselves trying to keep the pain buried and so we have very little leftover to give out.

In *Healing from Sexual Abuse*, Kathleen says, "No one can deny or repress the pain without personal damage" (6). Compare it to throwing refuse into a basement and locking the door. Over time the stench of the past will invade every relationship, filter into each thought, and eventually poison life itself.

So, how does a survivor deal with bits and pieces of memories that flash through her mind? Try to treat each one with kindness and trust. After all, this is your own subconscious asking to be acknowledged and accepted like a dear friend who has been lost for years finally making her way back home.

Welcome the memories that knock timidly on the door of your psyche and those that come rushing in like a flood. Record them as they come. Write them in a journal and pray over each one, asking the Lord to show you the truth. Writing like this brings clarity and insight, and at a future time rereading it will offer you confirmation and comfort. Trust the Lord to only bring back as much as you can handle.

I'll add a gentle word of warning here. Restoring suppressed memories is an organic process. These memories come to us; they filter in through our five senses. We must not take the initiative to dig up memories as if we were on a hunting expedition.

If the Lord does not bring suppressed memories to the surface, He may well intend for them to stay hidden away. Maybe the time isn't right, or maybe He doesn't want you to recall a certain incident. This is also a gift. Be thankful for His mercy.

Sexual experiences, even the ones we did not invite, involve our total selves—our mind, body, emotions, and even our souls. This explains why a certain song or scent, taste, phrase, or even an innocent touch from our husband can unleash an avalanche of unbidden, pain-filled memories.

Until we are healed, the images never really disappear. Sights like a smiling father swinging his daughter on the playground on a cool spring day can fill us with hot rage. Reactions like this are an indication that there are places inside us that still need to be healed. This is okay. It is not shameful. We never blame a person for being sick, so we should not accuse ourselves for the wounds we carry from being sexually abused.

Dear reader, haven't you been hurt enough? Robbed of so much? Should you continue to inflict pain on yourself by refusing to address the very reason you are suffering? We don't have to allow our past to continue to rule over us. Healing is possible for everyone, regardless of the type or extent of the trauma. What we experienced was illegal, unjust, cruel, and wretched.

Our personal healing has an undeniably spiritual component. We recognize the depths of human depravity in every case where a person is emotionally or physically exploited in order to meet another person's sexual or emotional need. We also understand that the solution isn't within ourselves or within another person.

Evil is like a raging beast that we are helpless to restrain or comprehend. It's too big for us. So we look far outside of all human conditions and limitations for complete restoration, seeking help and healing from the One who is greater, stronger, wiser, and purer.

We ask Him for deliverance and a new beginning, and we trust Him to administer justice. The group of survivors who have helped to fashion this book make no apology that we put our faith in the God revealed in Scripture. He is the One who has bound up our broken hearts. We believe it is His desire to set you free as He is doing for us.

The fact that you are reading this book may be because the Lord is urging you to press on. He may be quietly tugging on your heart not to give up, whispering that you are precious to Him and your life matters greatly, and that He has a wonderful plan for you. He knows you are finally ready to face the secret that have remained hidden, lurking in the unspoken recesses of your soul.

Please allow Him to bear your burdens and bind up your wounds. He's waiting to take your pain in exchange for healing, but the choice is yours.

Unlike our abusers, the Lord will never force Himself on you or make demands of you. He is gentle and kind and simply waits, with outstretched arms, for you to come to Him.

He will reach out to you every single day of your life, until your last breath. But why wait? Why go on trying to live as if what happened hasn't affected you? As if it doesn't cast its evil spell over your marriage and other significant relationships?

Stop pretending that you can live life fully and freely by ignoring all those memories festering inside. You have survived! Now it is time to face the pain in order to thrive for the rest of your life.

The Lord desires to make us whole in every area. He's the only One who can fully understand our pain and share our suffering. When we learn to trust Him with our brokenness and allow His Spirit to teach us His truth, He will redeem our past and realign our future.

There's no reason for you to wait another minute. Freedom, healing, and wholeness are available. Join hands with us. We have found the Lord to be trustworthy and faithful. He is healing us from sexual abuse, and if you will let

Him, He will do the same for you. When you take the first step of admitting your need and come to Jesus, your journey to wholeness begins.

✢  Are you ready to take the first step toward healing?

Not yet----------------Getting there------------------Yes, Yes, Yes!

## Requesting God's Help

"Lord, You know exactly what is bothering me. You understand my hurts and sorrow. You even know how hard it is for me to trust You. If You are real and if You love me, please help me and heal my wounds. Give me a new life. I need Your healing touch. I come to You now. In Jesus' name. Amen."

## Reflecting on Scripture

Read this section of Scripture, paying special attention to verse 29 (printed in bold.)

### Mark 5:25-29

25 A woman in the crowd had suffered for twelve years with constant bleeding.
26 She had suffered a great deal from many doctors, and over the years she had spent everything she had to pay them, but she had gotten no better. In fact, she had gotten worse.
27 She had heard about Jesus, so she came up behind him through the crowd and touched his robe.

²⁸ For she thought to herself, "If I can just touch his robe, I will be healed."
²⁹ **Immediately the bleeding stopped, and she could feel in her body that she had been healed of her terrible condition.**

Try to imagine the relief and joy this woman felt when her bleeding (a constant occurrence for twelve years) stopped. The original word, which is translated as bleeding, actually means "a well fed by a spring," a "wellspring," or a "fountain." It is often translated as "hemorrhaging." I think it's important to realize that our suffering sister had been bleeding heavily for a very long time.

We don't know what caused her to hemorrhage, but in the times when she lived, constant bleeding such as this was often believed to be the result of personal immoral behavior.[7] It was viewed as a plague, a result of immorality.

This certainly must have added a deep element of shame to our dear sister's life. Even if she had never acted in an immoral manner, others might have assumed she had.

The judgments of others can feel like a worse pain than an actual injury or illness. If you have felt misjudged or falsely accused by others, remember so did Jesus. He understands, and He knows how to heal this type of wound. The healing power of Jesus flowed out to this woman even without her having to ask.

Perhaps this precious woman had lived immorally. That didn't keep her from seeking healing. She might have been married and had an affair. Some survivors of sexual abuse go on to lead promiscuous lives or choose relationships which turn out to be abusive in some way.

In her book, *Door of Hope: Recognizing and Resolving the Pains of Your Past*, (Nashville: Thomas Nelson Publishers, 1995) Jan Frank writes, "The key to understanding the promiscuous response lies in the tie the victim makes between love and sex.

"Many have paired the two. Thus, in order to feel loved, she engages in sex. For many victims the incestuous incident was the only time she felt loved" (29).

When considering the possibility this woman's bleeding was a result of immorality, we need to acknowledge that sexual abuse is certainly immoral and survivors sometimes bear the consequences in their own body like the ongoing scourge of an incurable STD.

Another current example is the tragic superstitious belief, in some parts of the world, that sex with a virgin will cure AIDS. The result has been an increased number of girls being raped. These young girls lose their innocence and virginity and are often infected with the HIV virus.[8]

## Responding to God's Word

Other survivors may suffer from diseases resulting from abuse or from poor choices made in the aftermath of abuse. Some may struggle with sexual addictions or dysfunctions, or with the habit of masturbation. Each of these can bring confusion to the sexual union in marriage.

Some have faced pregnancy, which may have been followed by untold sorrow, accusation, and shame. They may have aborted their baby or given up the child for adoption. Any of these issues stemming from sexual abuse can cause a life to be undeniably altered.

Our dear woman may have been married, but her uncontrolled bleeding might have caused her husband to conclude she'd been unfaithful to him. Maybe she had experienced divorce. One thing is certain—this woman was considered unclean because of her bleeding and that meant she was forbidden to have contact with others. She was isolated and must have been very lonely.

It isn't necessary for us to know the actual cause of her bleeding in order to grasp the true significance of her story. The important part is that in her suffering she had the courage to go to Jesus and He healed her.

In light of the sobering possibilities of what may have caused this woman's suffering, let's again consider our verse, this time from the Amplified Bible.

**Mark 5:29**
> And immediately her flow of blood was dried up at the source, and [suddenly] she felt in her body that she was healed of her [distressing] ailment.

Please notice that our dear sister's condition was healed immediately at the source. The source of your suffering may be the abuse you experienced, or it may be the choices you have made in reaction to being sexually abused.

One survivor says that she struggles with self-condemnation. Whenever she makes a poor choice, it confirms to her that she is bad. Perhaps, like her, you've always believed you deserved the way you were treated, or put another way, "I must be a bad girl or this wouldn't happen."

You may be a person who takes responsibility for everything, and when anything bad happens, you believe that it's your fault. Or maybe you feel like everything always goes wrong and it's everyone's fault but yours.

Perceptions such as these lead to suffering. Whatever the source of your ongoing suffering, Jesus will heal you there. His healing isn't superficial; He goes deep to the root of the issue, to the very source of your pain.

When we reach out to Jesus and experience His healing, we know in our heart of hearts that we are forever changed.

## Releasing It All to the Lord

"Lord Jesus, we have many deep issues causing us ongoing pain. We may still be reacting to the abuse we experienced. We need You to heal us at the source of our suffering. Only You understand us completely; only You can heal us totally.

"Please, Lord, have mercy on us. Please heal us and let us feel in the deepest part of ourselves that we have been healed of our aliments and that our suffering has been dried up at the source. Amen."

Chapter **6**

## Swirling Waters

### Emily's Story

I raised my foot out of the whirlpool to inspect my toenails. "I can't believe that my feet actually look pretty."

"Oh, Emily, pedicures are glorious," Lindsay said. "It's unbelievable that you've never had one before."

Leaning back, I relaxed into the hot water jet that pulsed into the small of my back. Being with Lindsay was easy. I couldn't have asked for a sweeter roommate or more devoted friend to share the ups and downs of college life. And now, here she was again, right when I needed her to serve as my matron of honor.

I let out a contented sigh. "Spas just might be addicting."

"If you can afford them." Lindsay shrugged. "I only splurge for special occasions. And what could be more special than your wedding day?" She leaned close. "Unless, of course, it's your wedding night."

The sparkle in her eyes shot through me like fire as memories engulfed me. Still, I kept the expression of an expectant bride, full of wonder and joy. Thankfully, the swirling waters concealed the tremor that passed through my body while the unbidden images and unwanted emotions surged in.

~ ~ ~ ~ ~

I felt the jolt of being jerked from sleep by the sound of my bedroom door being slowly opened. Whenever Mom worked the night shift and Uncle Dean came to babysit, he would come into my room after my younger brother fell asleep.

As usual, I stayed motionless hoping with all my might that he'd change his mind and slither away. Instead he crept between my sheets. I was unsafe in my own bed.

My heart pounded like a wild caged animal. TRAPPED—unable to escape—I braced myself for yet another assault. In his whiny voice, Uncle Dean demanded that I touch him over and over again. I kept telling myself to just do it so it would be done and he'd leave. I held my breath against the smell of his spicy cologne as the weight of his sweaty, panting body shot searing pain through me.

When he was done, he reminded me that he would hurt me real bad, and my little brother too, if I ever told anyone about his secret visits. I believed him because I once watched him squeeze Fuzzy, my pet hamster, to death.

~ ~ ~ ~ ~

A jab from Lindsay brought me back to the present.

"Emily, are you even listening to me?"

I forced myself to focus on my dark-haired friend sitting next to me in the Jacuzzi. "Sorry."

"Dreaming about your wedding night?"

"Not really."

She inched closer. "Oh—you're scared aren't you?"

*Terrified.* "A little, I guess."

"Well, you're pretty special. You're only one of a few," she paused, "who's waited."

I tried to smile because she looked so proud of me.

"Don't worry, Emily," she said. "It's perfectly normal for you to feel uneasy about sex."

*There's nothing normal about what I feel.*

She gave me a knowing look. "I remember feeling un-certain, too."

*You have no idea.*

"But I can tell you—" Her voice lowered. "Making love with your husband is so special. You'll see. God designed it all perfectly, and it gets better all the time. Just remember, practice makes perfect." She winked.

I cringed. *How I wish sex wasn't part of being married.*

## Relating to the Story

* ❖ Can you relate to Emily? Did/does the thought of your wedding night fill you with dread?

Not at all--------------------Sometimes--------------------Totally

* ❖ Do you think marital intimacy is going to be difficult for Emily because of her experiences?

* ❖ Might it be or is it difficult for you?

Not at all--------------------------------------------------------Totally

* ❖ Will Emily's intimate relationships be affected if she refuses to deal with her past?

Yes---------------------------Maybe---------------------------No

* ❖ Does it or might it affect your intimate relationships? Your marriage? You?

Not at all ----------------------------------------------------Totally

❖ In order to have a satisfying sexual relationship in her marriage, do you think Emily will need to seek healing?

Yes---------------------------Maybe---------------------------No

❖ Do you need and want to be healed in this area of your life?

Not at all------------------------------------------------------Totally

## Recognizing the Issues ~ True Intimacy

If you've been affected by sexual abuse, you're not alone. Often it's a male family member or close friend who assaults younger, innocent females, or your mother might have been the one who abused you.

There are countless scenarios as varied as the evil intentions of individual depravity. Each one of us who has survived such abuse has her own story and personal reaction.

Some of us grew up to be promiscuous, while others, like Emily in this story, formed an aversion to sex. There is no denying that our lives and, therefore, our marriages, have been deeply impacted by our past experiences. We long for intimacy in our marriages but can't figure out how to make that happen. This hurts us, it is hard on our husbands, and it threatens our marriages.

One thing is certain for survivors. Our perception of human sexuality has been damaged. How can we rebuild a healthy understanding of God's design for sex?

Let's begin by acknowledging that our sexuality is a good and integral part of being human. This may be difficult for survivors to accept because what we experienced seemed so unnatural and perverted. It was! Sexual abuse is not sex as

God envisioned; in fact, it is an abhorrent distortion of God's holy design for sexuality.

Human sexuality involves our total selves—mind, body, emotions, and even our spirits. As stated before, this is one reason why sexuality is such a powerful force for good or evil.

As far back as the Garden of Eden, we see that the first area of personhood that was tainted when sin entered that perfect setting had to do with sexuality.

**Genesis 3:7-10** (emphasis added)

> At that moment their eyes were opened, and they suddenly *felt shame* at their *nakedness*. So they sewed fig leaves together to cover themselves.
>
> When the cool evening breezes were blowing, the man and his wife heard the LORD God walking about in the garden. So they *hid* from the LORD God among the trees.
>
> Then the LORD God called to the man, "Where are you?"
>
> He replied, "I heard you walking in the garden, so I hid. I was *afraid* because I was *naked*."

This Old Testament passage recounts how shame, fear, and hiding from God first entered the human experience because of disobedience. These basic reactions have been with us ever since. These reactions cause many to struggle with enjoying the good gift of sexual intimacy.

The concept that God designed sex as a gift might make you want to flee from such a Creator. Aside from the miracle of conception and giving birth to new life, sex might seem anything but good to you.

Please understand such views stem from being subjected to the lustful actions of others. Lust is sin and it is forbidden by the Lord (see Matthew 5:28).

When we refer to sexuality as God intended, we're talking about a pure and good gift shared by a husband and wife. This is redeemed and restored sexuality.

Our body has been fashioned to experience sexual pleasure in purity, but in order to do so we must have our emotions healed so that our physical bodies can be set free.

There are mysterious, God-designed benefits of the sexual union in marriage. When a husband and wife freely express their commitment and passion to each other during sex, it brings joy, satisfaction, comfort, and strength to them as a couple.

Their physical union affects other vital aspects of their relationship and life. In fact, when the sexual relationship is healthy, chances are everything in life will be better. The routine tasks of daily living will flow smoother, and we will gain perspective and courage from each other. We may find it easier to relate to our children, to interact with difficult co-workers, and to deal more effectively with stress.

If you ever wonder why you or your husband isn't doing a better job at work or with the kids or in areas related to faith, just consider how much or how little power flows from the sexual union you share.

For some married couples, sharing intimately isn't automatic or easy. To begin with, men and women are so different in the way their bodies, minds, and desires react and respond. The husband may want sex more often than the wife. However, some women find a deep need for more frequent sexual contact.

It's been suggested that women may not have what we call a *sex drive*, but rather a *relational drive*. That means our desire for sexual intimacy is primarily about our longing for affection, attention, and closeness from our husbands. Our sex drive may have more to do with maintaining the relationship than it has to do with wanting physical intercourse.

For survivors seeking healing, it is helpful to analyze how our attitudes about sexuality in marriage have been impacted by our experiences. Is sex repulsive? Do we view males in general, or our husband specifically, as only wanting one thing? Is it our secret opinion that all men want to use women for their own selfish gratification?

Or did we move from being sexually abused to employing sex as a means to control, hurt, or demean men? Maybe sexual conquest has become a way to seek validation of our worth whenever we feel insecure or threatened. We may have developed a need for constant affirmation through lots of sex, or we might be trapped in a destructive sexual addiction.

One survivor describes herself as sexually free before marriage, often acting aggressive in initiating sexual contact with men. She thought sex was exciting and enjoyed these encounters, so she assumed she liked sex.

When she married, she suddenly felt obligated to meet her husband's sexual needs and she found sex to be distasteful. This marital commitment actually reminded her of the years when she was abused and had no choice but to meet the sexual demands of her abuser. She still struggles in this area of her marriage.

In order to move toward healing, each survivor has to acknowledge that the experience of sexual abuse has impacted her intimate relationships. This makes perfect sense because the part of us that was awakened and attacked had to do with our own sexuality.

God's intention was for us to slowly unwrap the gift of our own sexuality and discover sexual union in the context of a lifelong, committed love relationship of mutual trust, tenderness, and respect. He designed this as a good gift—one that delights Him so much that the fruit of this relationship is often new life. But instead of experiencing this natural unfolding of human sexuality at the appropriate times in the context of a life-long, mutually exclusive relationship, sexual awareness was thrust upon many of us much too early and in inappropriate and damaging ways.

Experiencing sexual abuse might be compared to being run over by a huge, roaring locomotive which leaves us broken and barely alive. The truth remains, however, that the love of God is more powerful than the destruction caused by others. He knows how to take the scattered pieces of our broken hearts and mend them. In fact, He is the one who makes all things new. Don't you want to have a new start? This can happen, but it is not by denying the past because, as we've said before, our past is actually a part of who we are today.

Realizing that our sexual struggles in marriage stem from our abuse may come to us in different ways. I (Sue) acknowledged it when, as a young bride, I discovered that my body would shut down during sexual arousal.

After prayer and consideration, I realized that this was linked to my sexual assault as a ten-year-old child. I ran away from my abuser when he inappropriately awakened my sexual response. It scared me. I didn't like anything about the encounter. I felt sick to my stomach and thought I might throw up.

Years later, my body still stopped responding at that same point of arousal even though I was a happily married woman and deeply in love with my husband. That's when I admitted that I needed help. It seemed wrong to me that my past should rob my husband and me of the pleasure of a great sexual relationship in our marriage. I wanted to be healed.

Now, after years of enjoying the pleasures of marital intimacy, I am so thankful I faced the effects of being sexually abused and that the Lord healed me.

We understand that dealing with our painful past isn't easy, but believe us when we say that it is more dangerous and damaging to ignore the truth than it is to face it. God wants to heal your body, soul, and spirit. He wants you and your husband to experience a mutually enjoyable, intimate relationship in your marriage. So, even if you feel hesitant to delve into past pain and you can't do it for yourself, do it for your husband and do it for your marriage. In doing so, you will also reap the benefits.

## Requesting God's Help

The following prayer is for readers who are married.

"Oh, Lord, I want to be whole. You know my attitude about sex, and I choose to surrender it to You. I want to see sex as You see it—as a good gift to me and to my husband. Please bring us healing. I want this relationship to be good for both of us. Help me to be understanding toward my husband and his sexual needs; help him to be understanding toward me. Please bring healing and strength to our marriage. Teach me what I need to know. Give me wisdom and grace and most of all courage as I take this journey with You. Amen."

The following prayer is for readers who are not married.

"Lord, You know my view about sex. I'm asking You to change my heart and mind and help me to see sexuality as You do. You know where I need healing. I give You all my brokenness and pain and ask You to bring me wholeness. Please heal me so that if it's Your plan for me to marry or remarry, I will be able to enjoy a healthy and satisfying intimate relationship with my spouse. Amen."

## Reflecting on Scripture

Read this section of Scripture, paying special attention to verse 30 (printed in bold).

### Mark 5:25-30

25 A woman in the crowd had suffered for twelve years with constant bleeding.

26 She had suffered a great deal from many doctors, and over the years she had spent everything she had to pay them, but she had gotten no better. In fact, she had gotten worse.

27 She had heard about Jesus, so she came up behind him through the crowd and touched his robe.

28 For she thought to herself, "If I can just touch his robe, I will be healed."

29 Immediately the bleeding stopped, and she could feel in her body that she had been healed of her terrible condition.

30 **Jesus realized at once that healing power had gone out from him, so he turned around in the crowd and asked, "Who touched my robe?"**

This verse is different from all the ones before it because it isn't describing the woman or her condition or her thoughts. This verse is about Jesus. It tells us His response when healing power flowed out from Him.

Last time, we read about what our precious woman felt in her body. Today we'll consider how Jesus reacted to what He felt.

Notice that Jesus is aware that healing power has gone out from Him. This means that healing power belongs to Him. Healing is in Him. Healing is His. We do not have the power to heal ourselves. No, Jesus alone has the power to heal us at our point of need. He is the source of healing. That's why we come to Him to be healed.

Let's set the stage by considering the circumstances that surrounded Jesus when "he turned around in the crowd and asked, 'Who touched my clothes?'" First, picture a huge gathering of people. The woman had to push her way through these people.

Think about this scene from the viewpoint of Jesus. He was the reason for the crowd. If He had not been there, none of those people would have been there. The masses wanted Him. He was the center of attention.

People pressed in on Jesus from every side, and they all wanted something from Him. There were lots of desperate folks clamoring for His attention.

Perhaps some just wanted to hear Jesus teach. Others, like our dear woman, wanted to touch Him to be healed. I'm sure many begged Jesus to grant their requests. Did they shout, yell, and call out His name? I bet it was noisy, with that many people all intent on getting to Jesus. Did His disciples act as bodyguards? Was it their job to try to keep the crowd under control?

By reading about what happened before this event in Mark 5:1-24, we learn the following:

* ❖ Jesus returned, by boat, to Galilee from the land of the Gerasenes.

* ❖ While in the land of the Gerasenes, Jesus healed a very violent man who was possessed by many demons.

* ❖ Jesus sent the demons into a herd of two thousand pigs.

* ❖ All the pigs plunged down a steep hillside into the lake where they drowned.

❖ The people of that area begged Jesus to leave.

❖ Jesus traveled back across the Sea of Galilee and was met by a throng of people.

❖ Then Jairus, a leader of the local synagogue, fell at the feet of Jesus. He begged Jesus to come and lay His hands on his little daughter who was dying so she would be healed.

❖ Jesus went with Jairus.

❖ A large crowd followed and pressed in on Him.

This is the point in the story when the bleeding woman is numbered among the crowd of people who are pressing in on Jesus. I'm sure He is moving slowly since there are so many people. He is on his way to the home of Jairus. There, a little girl is dying and a desperate father is urging Jesus to come and help. Jesus has a task. He is on a mission. There is no time to waste.

Think for a moment about how you would feel if this were your child. Wouldn't you want Jesus to hurry? Maybe you would even try to push people aside in order to help Jesus move more quickly. Life and death are at stake, but there is hope because Jesus has responded to your request and He is on His way to heal your daughter.

I am amazed that Jesus didn't tell everyone to leave Him alone, to stop grabbing at Him, and to quit pushing! Have you ever felt like everyone wanted something from you? How do you react?

Jesus isn't bothered by the crowd of people or by the depth of their needs. He doesn't rebuke or ignore them. He is full of compassion. The requests of the people matter to Him; He loves and cares for them.

At this moment, there is an urgent matter that needs His attention, and Jesus is moving forward. I imagine He is going as quickly as He can to heal the daughter of a very important man. This is when Jesus feels healing power leave Him.

What does Jesus do? He doesn't ignore the fact and keep going. No, He turns around in the crowd. This means Jesus stopped. He stopped what He was doing. He stopped going where He was going. He stopped and turned around.

Why? Because He knew that someone had reached out in faith and received healing. Faith always catches the attention of the Lord. It mattered to Him that our dear sister touched Him. She mattered to Him. So, He asked, "Who touched my clothes?"

## Responding to God's Word

You may think that Jesus is too busy to care about you and your relationships. You might even think that your struggle is too personal to discuss with the Lord. "He has other things to do, more important matters to tend to."

Maybe you have the idea that the Lord understands others but not you because you are not worthy. You are used to being overlooked—to having others dismiss you and disregard your feelings and needs.

None of those thoughts are based on truth. The Lord carefully fashioned you in your mother's womb, and He has a good plan for your life. Jesus loves you. Your suffering matters to Him. You are not interrupting Him when you ask Him to help you. He will respond when you reach out for Him in faith. So, do it; do it now!

## Releasing It All to the Lord

"Lord Jesus, thank You that You are never too busy for me! Thank You that my problems are not insignificant to You. What concerns me, concerns You.

"Thank You that You don't have more urgent matters to attend to. Thank You that You want me to come to You with all that is in my heart; all that is on my mind; all my struggles, heartaches, and disappointments. Thank You that Your focus is on me and that I can lay all of my requests before You. Please heal me, Lord. Amen."

Below is an additional prayer for married readers.

"Lord, God, please heal my marriage. You know where we need Your help and healing. I want our entire marriage, and especially our intimate relationship, to be healthy and enjoyable, but that can't happen unless You work a miracle. Please, Lord, I'm begging You for a miracle. Amen."

*Chapter* 7

# Questions

## *Shawnda Rae's Story*

Shawnda Rae came in from work, switched on the TV, and went into the kitchen to prepare dinner. She started to chop carrots, but a moment later, she looked up at the TV screen and felt her stomach lurch. As if pulled by an invisible force, she left the kitchen and slumped onto the sofa. Her hand trembled as she pushed the volume button on her remote and squinted at the TV screen through a blur of tears.

"The body of yet another young girl was found in a remote section of Taylor Nature Preserve early this morning. As in the case of the other young victim, discovered last week, the body showed signs of severe trauma. . . ."

The tremor in her hands swept through her, and soon Shawnda Rae's whole body shook in a violent reaction to the news report. Then, the room where she sat seemed to dissolve around her as a distant memory transported her back to her own childhood.

~ ~ ~ ~ ~

Eight-year-old Shawnda Rae knew she was fast. Since pre-school, she always won the races at school. Now, she could even outrun all the boys in the third-grade. But this day Shawnda Rae wasn't trying to run faster than her classmates. She ran, with all her might, to get away from Charles, her mother's boyfriend.

Shawnda Rae's heart pounded in her ribs. Her sneakers stomped the dry pine needles covering the ground as she plunged through the forest of Taylor Nature Preserve. She gasped as she dodged trees and avoided roots. *Go, go, don't stop. Don't stop.*

With all her might, Shawnda Rae ran. She ran for her life.

At first, she heard no other sound. *He's not coming after me.* The thought filled her with new energy as she sprinted on.

But then, behind her, came the unmistakable sharp crack of a branch being snapped by a heavy foot and the uncontrolled swearing of an angry man. *He's coming!*

Panic compelled her to press on. *Faster—faster. Away, away, away—get away.* Shawnda Rae did all she could do, but in the end, she lost the race.

Back on the sofa in her own living room, Shawnda Rae pulled her knees toward her belly and groaned. The memory tightened its grip. Unwillingly she relived the terror of being caught and abused.

As if they were playing a game of chase, Charles grabbed her braids and threw her to the ground with a cruel and crushing laugh. "You think you can run from me, you little whore?"

His heavy boot pressed hard into her stomach. "I'll show you who you're messing with."

He unbuckled his belt with one hand and yanked her sweatpants down with the other . . .

~ ~ ~ ~ ~

Twenty minutes later, when Shawnda Rae's husband, Martin, came into their home, he saw his wife curled up on the sofa, trembling. Before he approached her, he called out softly. "I'm home, Shawny-girl. You okay?"

She moaned.

He dropped to his knees beside her and stroked her head. "It's okay. I'm here."

She locked eyes with him, and drew comfort from the understanding she saw reflected there. "Hold me," she whimpered.

Martin scooted onto the sofa and gathered his wife in his arms. He rocked her. "Let's pray."

She swallowed and nodded. *Yes, prayer, that's what I need.*

"Lord," her husband said, his voice quivering, "please comfort my wife. She's suffering. Help her. Take away these tormenting memories. You see how she's hurting. Just wipe them away. You said that You make all things new, Jesus, so loosen the power of these images and set my Shawny-girl free. Please, Lord, I'm begging You. Please."

Shawnda Rae felt the warmth of her husband's tears hit the side of her neck. The strength of his powerful love wrapped her in comfort. Suddenly, she wanted to reassure him, and so she took hold of his hand as she whispered, "Jesus, thank You for my husband. It's so good to be loved. But what about that little girl, Lord? What about her family? Why did You let her suffer? Why didn't You rescue her?"

Her shoulders began to shake as she sobbed. "And why do I still have these horrible flashbacks after so many years? Where were You, Lord, when that little girl needed Your help? Where were You when I cried out to You? Won't the memories ever leave? I need You to heal me, Jesus. Why do these things have to happen? It's so evil and it hurts for so long. Why, Lord? Why?"

Shawnda Rae quieted and turned to look into her husband's face. He leaned over to plant a kiss on her forehead.

She touched his cheek. "Don't leave me, ever. Okay? Just hold me. Please hold me."

He held her tight. As he did, he rocked her and hummed, "Jesus loves me, this I know. For the Bible tells me so . . ."

## Relating to the Story

❖ Do you have strong reactions when you hear reports of child sexual abuse?

Never--------------------Sometimes----------------------Always

❖ Can you relate to this story in any of the following ways?

| Need for comfort | Physical reaction | Questions for God |
|---|---|---|
| Flashbacks of my abuse | Overcome with emotion | Praying with someone |

## Recognizing the Issues ~ Ask the Lord

Survivors have questions. Questions like:

❖ "If God is a God of love, why did He let that happen to me?"

❖ "When I cried out to Him, why didn't He answer me?"

❖ "Why me?"

❖ "How could He allow such things?"

❖ "Was I being punished for something I did wrong?"

Such questions are legitimate, yet they often remain unasked and, therefore, unanswered. We end up taking them into adulthood with us where we either deny that we have questions to ask of God or where we form our own conclusions about the answers based on our ongoing experiences. Some try to diminish such questions as unimportant or rebuke themselves for even having them. *I shouldn't question God.*

The truth is that God is big enough to handle every single one of our questions. If we really want His answers, we must be willing to ask Him each one of our honest questions. This may make you feel uncomfortable, but I'm praying you'll push past your discomfort.

It's time to move forward. Seeking answers to our questions is so central to healing that we will take this chapter to lay the biblical foundation for questioning God and the next chapter to show you how to personally apply it.

## Requesting God's Help

"Lord, it scares me to even think about the questions I have about my sexual abuse. I'm so ashamed. I think that maybe I shouldn't ever talk about it to anyone—especially not You.

"Maybe You're punishing me, and if I ask You these questions, things will get really bad for me. Even having these thoughts seems wrong.

"Then again, You let it happen and that has caused me to have a lot of ugly questions about what You are like. It seems like You can't be good and loving and let that happen to me. I'm confused. I need You to help me figure out what to do with the questions that have been brewing inside me for so long. Amen."

## Reflecting on Scripture

Read our Bible passage is printed below. Pay special attention to verse 31 printed in bold.

### Mark 5:25-31
²⁵ A woman in the crowd had suffered for twelve years with constant bleeding.

²⁶ She had suffered a great deal from many doctors, and over the years she had spent everything she had to pay them, but she had gotten no better. In fact, she had gotten worse.
²⁷ She had heard about Jesus, so she came up behind him through the crowd and touched his robe.
²⁸ For she thought to herself, "If I can just touch his robe, I will be healed."
²⁹ Immediately the bleeding stopped, and she could feel in her body that she had been healed of her terrible condition.
³⁰ Jesus realized at once that healing power had gone out from him, so he turned around in the crowd and asked, "Who touched my robe?"
³¹ **His disciples said to him, "Look at this crowd pressing around you. How can you ask, 'Who touched me?'"**

Let's review. Up to this point, we've read about the woman, her condition, and the actions she took. We've also seen how Jesus responded. Now, we'll look at verse 31 which records the disciples' reaction when Jesus stops to ask, "Who touched my robe?" This one verse is actually made up of two sentences and we'll consider them individually.

**His disciples said to him, "Look at this crowd pressing around you."**

Do you ever feel lost in a crowd? As if you have no value? Have you ever longed to matter to someone, to have someone notice you? What about God? Do you think that He has more important things to do than to listen to you when you pray or to care about the details of your life?

This story shows us that Jesus takes notice of each individual. The disciples saw a massive crowd of people, but Jesus sought out one specific person. Someone in that crowd had touched His robe in faith, believing that when they did, they would be healed. And when Jesus felt healing power flow out from Him, He wanted to talk to that person face-to-face. He wanted to acknowledge that person. He was seeking a relationship.

We matter to the Lord. The things that concern us, concern Him. Others may try to convince us that God is too busy to care about us and our individual needs. You may have heard comments similar to today's verse. "There are such pressing needs in this world, don't bother the Lord. He's busy with more important matters." This passage proves that statements like that are not based on what is true about God.

Jesus, who is God in the flesh, cared enough to take the effort to seek out our dear sister. From the little to the big things, the Lord cares for each of us. He is our good Father and His eye is upon us. When we hurt, He draws near.

### "How can you ask, 'Who touched me?'"

Read the parallel account of this story to gain more information.

#### Luke 8:45-46

"Who touched me?" Jesus asked. Everyone denied it, and Peter said, "Master, this whole crowd is pressing up against you." But Jesus said, "Someone deliberately touched me, for I felt healing power go out from me."

We see that Peter is identified as the disciple who responded when Jesus stopped in the middle of something that seemed urgent to ask the seemingly unimportant question, "Who touched my clothes?" Peter doesn't appear to be asking Jesus an honest question. To me Peter's question sounds incredulous as if he's thinking something like, "It's impossible to know in a crowd this size." His question might also be along the lines of rebuking Jesus for asking such a ridiculous question at such an inopportune time.

## Responding to God's Word

Earlier in this chapter, we challenged you to bring your questions to God. In the next chapter we'll show you how to do that. We've stated that it's okay to question the Lord and to ask Him the "why" questions. Here, Peter is questioning Jesus. While Peter is not asking Jesus a personal question, we do see an example of how Jesus responds when questioned.

In light of the personal questions you might have, take a careful look at how Jesus responded to Peter. Read the passage recorded in Luke to answer these questions.

❖ How would you describe Jesus' response to Peter's question?

| Explains Himself | Takes time to respond | Ignores the question |
|---|---|---|
| Offers more information | Puts Peter in his place | Makes Peter feel stupid |

❖ What does this reveal about how the Lord responds to questions?

| It makes Him angry | He helps us to understand | He allows questions |
|---|---|---|
|  |  |  |

Even when we ask questions because we don't understand why the Lord does what He does, we see He is willing to respond.

It's also significant to consider what Jesus doesn't do when Peter questions Him. He doesn't rebuke Peter. He doesn't tell Peter that his question is stupid. And Jesus isn't defensive. He doesn't put Peter in his place by saying, "Hey, I'm God. Why are you questioning Me?" Jesus didn't take offense.

This teaches us about how God views the questions we ask when we just don't understand. He kindly offers us insight, shows us new information, and expands our perspective.

We see that Jesus isn't put off by Peter's question. There's no indication that the Lord is annoyed. No, Jesus answers Peter while staying focused on discovering the person who had touched Him. Peter's question doesn't seem to be central to what God was doing at that moment, yet Jesus took the time to respond.

Notice that it's one single woman and her healing that is occupying the heart and mind of Jesus. It's not the crowd or the sick girl or her desperate father, and it's not the dubious disciples. Peter's question mattered to Jesus, because Peter mattered to Jesus.

We also see that Jesus is still seeking the one person, among thousands, who had managed to get close enough to Him to reach out in faith and touch His robe. You matter to Jesus like that. Even when there are countless needs and innumerable prayers, He still hears your voice, sees your pain, and stops to listen.

In this passage, I think that Jesus wasn't really asking His disciples to answer the question, "Who touched me?" Since Jesus is God, He already knew who had reached out in faith and touched Him. We witness the kindness and compassion of Jesus when He refrains from singling out our dear woman. Instead, He gives her the opportunity to identify herself. It was as if He was saying to our dear sister, "Who are you? Where are you? Please come and talk to Me."

## Releasing It All to the Lord

"Lord, thank You that You don't mind if I ask questions. Please teach me how to pour out my sorrow, doubts, questions, and pain to You. Thank You that You want to hear from me. You know me and what I am thinking. You know what I have thought about being sexually abused. There's so much I don't understand. I just come to You now. Please, Lord, speak to me. Amen."

*Chapter* **8**

# Too Ashamed

## *Carol's Story*

We sat on folding chairs in a tight circle, eight women gathered for a small group discussion. The afternoon sun streamed through the cabin window and the scent of pine filled the air. I wished I could stay another day or two.

Our leader, Lara, sat to my left and quieted us.

"Well, ladies," she said, "I've got to say that my favorite part of this retreat has been getting to know each of you during our small group times. I feel like we've grown close, and I'm sad that it's our last meeting."

She took a breath. "Okay, so what did you think about the message we just heard on forgiveness?"

She turned to me. "Carol, do you have any comments?"

My heart began to race, but I kept my voice steady. "Well, I'm thankful that I've been forgiven."

She smiled. "Me, too."

Relief as tangible as a cool shower on a sweltering day washed over me.

Lara glanced at the other ladies in the circle. "Any other thoughts?"

Tina who seemed to be in her late twenties, with curly blond hair, shifted in her seat. "To be honest, I'm struggling with what the speaker said. I mean, what if there is someone who just doesn't deserve our forgiveness?" Tina stopped and looked down at her lap.

I felt grateful that no one said, "None of us deserves forgiveness," even though it's true. Tina looked really troubled.

Lara leaned toward her. "Go on, Tina."

Tina's left eye twitched slightly and her face flushed. She glanced around the circle; her eyes seemed to plead for understanding. "What if . . ." Tina stopped again and took a deep breath. "The real problem for me isn't just trying to forgive someone who's hurt you, it's the concept that the Lord is also called our heavenly—father."

"And that image is difficult for you?" Lara asked.

"Yes." Tina almost spat the word. "It's probably easy if you had a decent dad, but my father is a total hypocrite." She paused and we all waited. "He's a pastor in a small town in Idaho. Everyone thinks he's so holy—but I know the truth."

Again, my heart began to pump franticly. I felt the urge to run from the room. *What's she going to say? What if we're all expected to tell our secrets?*

I liked the women and all, but there was no way on earth I wanted to make that type of disclosure.

Tina's tears started. Lara rose to set a box of tissues at her feet. Tina took one and then, as if a floodgate had burst open, her story just gushed out.

"My earliest memory is of sitting with my father on our special chair. It was a brown lounge chair with a long foot area to stretch out your legs. We used a soft blue blanket to cover ourselves whenever we sat there."

My throat tightened as I listened to Tina. She spoke softly, so it was hard to hear her, but I think we all sensed how difficult it must be for her to talk about such personal things. So when the others leaned in to listen, I did too. *I don't want them to think I don't care.*

"My father always whispered to me. He said I was so special. I have three younger sisters, but he said I was his very favorite daughter. He would caress and stroke me under the blanket."

She looked up, her eyes suddenly blazing, her voice rising. "It sounds so sweet, doesn't it? But when I think back, I realize that I never wore panties during our playtimes. There was always bare skin—for both of us. I was so little, so innocent." Her voice trailed off.

The other ladies responded with revulsion and so did I. Even as memories of my Aunt June flashed through my mind. She also told me I was her favorite. I fought hard to push away the images and rising panic.

*That's over. It doesn't affect me now.* I clicked my tongue in sympathy and dabbed my eyes as Tina continued to describe the ugly details of her past.

"My mother was totally emotionally distant; she never hugged any of us or said anything kind. I never remember her telling me that she loved me. Even now, she's a hard and cold woman. I think she hated being the wife of a pastor. So when we were growing up, the only attention any of us got came from our father. That filled a need, you know? But I feel so guilty that I needed and even liked the affection he showed me."

Several of the others reached for tissues as Tina kept talking. "I've never shared this with anyone," she sobbed. "My own husband doesn't even know." She paused. "I'm sorry to be dumping it all on you."

That's when we reassured her that it was all right—that we cared about her and her pain. What I really wanted to do was get up and get out of that place. I didn't want to listen to any more. Every sentence Tina spoke stirred up bitterness and anger inside me.

Then, my heart started to quiver the way it does when God is speaking to me. *Oh, Lord, don't ask me to share my story. I just can't!*

I felt so embarrassed that it was women who abused me. First, Aunt June, and then a counselor at summer camp. It went on for many years until I grew taller and stronger and met my Aunt June with a baseball bat when she came into my bedroom. I told her, "If you try to touch me now or ever again, I'll use this to protect myself."

Some of our group knelt beside Tina, patting her knees or rubbing her back as she talked. Many cried. I followed their lead and crossed over to stand near Tina so I wouldn't be the only one still sitting in a chair.

Inside, my heart churned. The Lord knew that I'd sworn long ago that I'd never ever let anyone know about my past. I'd locked it away when I married and went on with my new life.

Even though I knew that my inability to enjoy intimacy with my husband strained our marriage, I just couldn't tell him. I would not let it out, now or ever. It would stay hidden away. When Aunt June finally died—then, I'd be free.

Tina blew her nose and took a deep breath before she said haltingly, "So as a little girl I viewed myself as extra special—chosen. And all the people at church and in our town loved my dad. They still do. And I was his favorite.

"Even in elementary school when my playtimes with Daddy happened in the middle of the night and resulted in physical pain, I still thought it was just the way daddies and daughters played and showed love to each other."

She paused and glanced at us; her eyes full of fury. "He's such a skillful liar. He carefully manipulated me from when I was so young. But as I grew and learned the truth, I felt so disgusted, so filled with shame. And I became fearful of getting married. I didn't want to have any daughters, because the man I married might hurt them. Why did God let that happen to me?"

I felt like I couldn't listen to another word. Once, I almost spoke—but then my feeble attempt was drowned by Tina's sobs. Sweat covered my neck and back. I thought I might faint. *I wish she'd stop talking so this would all be over.* I'm not sure how much more she said or how long it took. I couldn't listen. I blocked out the rest.

No one noticed when I went back to my chair and put my head in my hands as if I was praying. They all surrounded Tina with loving support, and when it was all over, she looked relieved as if a heavy weight had been taken from her. But I felt worse than I had felt in years. When I started to sob, they all thought I cried for Tina.

## Relating to the Story

* ❖ Have you ever heard someone else speak about his or her abuse?

* ❖ How did it make you feel?

| Scared to tell my story | Wanted to tell my story | Not sure how I felt |
|---|---|---|

* ❖ Talking about topics like sexual abuse is becoming more common. Do you think this is good or bad? Why?

## Recognizing the Issues ~ Listening Prayer

Dear Ones, we have reached the point in our journey toward healing when it's time to ask the long hidden, unasked questions that stem from being sexually abused. Unanswered questions such as these can turn into deep doubts and false theology.

When we reach unfounded conclusions about God based on our own answers to the questions we have, we are often misled, mistaken, and deceived.

In our last chapter, we established that it is okay to ask God questions. This chapter will explain a way to bring our questions to the Lord and how to hear His reply.

## Requesting God's Help

"Lord Jesus, You know the questions I have even before I ask them. In fact, You are aware of the questions that I have not yet acknowledged. Please help me to identify the questions that have arisen from my hurtful experience. Please give me courage to talk to someone safe. Show me that person. Help me to see clearly, and give me courage to deal with the issues in my own heart. Amen."

## Reflecting on Scripture

This chapter is like a pause in our story about the woman who bled. Since we're focusing on talking to and hearing from God, it will be helpful to focus on a specific example of prayer that we find in the Bible. In the next chapter we'll return to the story of the bleeding woman.

We can learn a lot by reading about others who prayed with total honesty—people who held nothing back. They just poured out everything hidden in their hearts. Some did it in verbal prayers; others did it in writing. Either way works. You may be drawn to one type of praying more than to another. In the psalms, David used writing to express this type of open communication with the Lord Almighty.

Hannah's prayer is a clear example of a woman praying out loud in her deep distress. Let's study her prayer to gain insight about praying with an honest heart.

## A Look at Hannah's Prayer

## (A true story from 1 Samuel chapters 1 & 2)

Before reading Hannah's prayer, let's consider some background that explains why she is so upset. First, she can't have children. This has caused her heart to break. Second, she has to share her husband with another wife named Peninnah who is able to have babies.

Hannah's husband truly loved her, and maybe that is why the other wife was so mean to her. These two verses sum it up. "Peninnah would taunt Hannah and make fun of her because the LORD had kept her from having children. Year after year it was the same—Peninnah would taunt Hannah as they went to the Tabernacle. Each time, Hannah would be reduced to tears and would not even eat" (1 Samuel 1:6-7).

Later in this chapter we will address the fact that it is the Lord who closed Hannah's womb. Set that aside for now as you concentrate on Hannah's prayer. These verses describe Hannah's dysfunctional family. There was no peace in their home. The relationships were unhealthy, and day after day Hannah lived with a woman who verbally abused her. It affected her. She felt depressed, she cried all the time, and she couldn't even eat. In this state of mind, Hannah goes into the Tabernacle to pray. A priest named Eli overhears her as she prays.

> Hannah was in deep anguish, crying bitterly as she prayed to the LORD. And she made this vow: "O LORD of Heaven's Armies, if you will look upon my sorrow and answer my prayer and give me a son, then I will give him back to you. He will be yours for his entire lifetime, and as a sign that he has been dedicated to the LORD, his hair will never be cut."

As she was praying to the LORD, Eli watched her. Seeing her lips moving but hearing no sound, he thought she had been drinking. "Must you come here drunk?" he demanded. "Throw away your wine!"

"Oh no, sir!" she replied, "I haven't been drinking wine or anything stronger. But I am very discouraged, and I was pouring out my heart to the LORD. Don't think I am a wicked woman! For I have been praying out of great anguish and sorrow" (1 Samuel 1:10-16).

## Responding to God's Word

❖ Please identify any words in this passage that describe Hannah's feelings.

❖ How does Hannah express her emotions?

When Hannah talks to God, she doesn't pretend that all is well. In fact, we see that she's in great anguish as she tells the Lord all about how she feels.

❖ Have you ever prayed in total honesty like Hannah did?
Never---------------------A few times------------------Always do

You may have been raised in a family where expressing feelings was not allowed. Denying emotions is easier than identifying them. If this describes you, ask the Lord to help you to access and express your true feelings. Hannah's prayer serves as a great example of someone who is in touch with her feelings and pours them out before the Lord.

Now, it's time to explain how to pour out your heart to the Lord. This is when you'll ask all the questions you may have about your sexual abuse like, "Lord, where were You when I was being abused?"

By following the suggestions in this chapter you will find the freedom to ask all that is in your heart and to give God the opportunity to answer. Let Him speak, and listen to what He has to say. This requires total honesty, some focused time, and a place where you are safe from interruptions.

I can't encourage you strongly enough to actually take the time to do this exercise. It can be life changing. Think of all the years you may still have to live, and ask yourself if you can spare one hour to see if God is actually alive and eager to meet with you. I assure you He is, but you have to discover this for yourself. Do it for yourself and for the close relationships you have or hope to have in the future.

## Releasing It All to the Lord

This time I'm not writing out a prayer because you'll be saying your own prayers. This requires courage but results in freedom. When you talk to the Lord, you don't need to recite a prayer written by someone else or say things in a certain way. Your heart attitude matters most. Think of how honestly Hannah prayed. God heard her. He answered. Being real with God may seem scary, but it's what He requires.

After all, He already knows everything. He knows all about our abuse, what we've thought about Him, and how we've reacted. Nothing will surprise or offend Him. We are the ones who are often shocked by the questions that reside deep within our souls.

## Listening Prayer Points

How do we actually pray so God will answer, and listen so we can hear? One way is called "Listening Prayer." I've heard it said that God gave us two ears and one mouth because we should listen twice as much as we should talk.

This is certainly true when it comes to praying. When we spill out all that's pressed down inside of us, we create room to listen to God's voice. Praying like this is summed up in two parts. First, is the honest pouring out; then, is the quiet taking in. You can offer up silent prayers or shout loudly. Whatever works best for you is what is best.

I think it's easiest to use writing to pray this way, so I'm strongly suggesting that you use a journal or notebook as a place to write your prayers to the Lord. This is also where you can record what He says and reveals to you. I'm going to assume that you've taken my suggestion and will be writing out your prayers/questions to God.

Now, let me say a word about hearing the voice of God. Praying is a spiritual conversation. God is Spirit and so is the Evil One who is also called Satan. Not every voice we hear is God's voice.

Remember earlier when we talked about taking every thought captive? Some of our thoughts are simply our own, others are from God, and some may come from Satan. One way to determine the source of a given thought is to ask: "Does this bring me life or death?" "Am I being encouraged or discouraged, empowered or accused?"

The Lord's voice always brings life, encouragement, and power. Yes, sometimes He will correct us and ask us to repent. When this happens, He is very specific about what it is He is asking of us.

Satan accuses, blames, and casts heavy loads of guilt on us. He may also spread vague feelings of inadequacy without being specific about what it is we need to do to move toward righteousness. In contrast, when the Lord brings conviction, He is specific about what we are doing that displeases Him and about what He is asking us to do. Knowing this will help you to determine if what you are hearing is from the Lord who loves you or from the Evil One who has come to kill, rob, and destroy.[9]

If you feel like you would benefit from having someone help you pray in this way, there are those who specialize in this type of praying. For more information go to: Theophostic Prayer Ministry, www.theophostic.com.

Or, if during your prayer time you find yourself so troubled that you can't continue, please stop and seek the help of a professional Christian counselor or pastor.

Maybe you don't think you even know how to pray. Well, prayer is simply talking to God and listening to what He says in response. Since the Lord knows our every thought before we think it and our every word before we speak it,[10] writing our thoughts out to Him is a type of praying. It can aid us in expressing what is deep inside and help us in hearing God's reply.

You might not be used to doing this, but it isn't hard to do. Here are some steps to take as you prepare for your own time of prayer.

* Give yourself time, at least one hour, when you are not rushed or pressed by other demands.

* Find a private place where you feel safe. A lock on the door may help you feel secure and ensure that you won't be interrupted.

❖ You may not be able to do this at home and might consider going to a friend's house or a prayer room at a church.

❖ Take a Bible along with you. I'm suggesting a modern, easy to read translation like the New Living Translation or New International Version.

❖ Have something to write in—a journal or notebook, and a pen or pencil. Even if you prefer a verbal dialogue, take something to write in so you can record what God says. You will find it a source of comfort and encouragement in the future.

❖ Take along tissues and water to drink. A watch or timer might be useful to keep track of time.

❖ Begin by asking the Lord to speak and to help you to only hear His voice. Ask Him to protect you from any misleading, false or confusing thoughts.

Once you're settled and ready to begin, turn in your Bible and read Lamentations 3 or Psalm 55. These sections are also printed in the appendix of this book.

Both of these passages are examples of a person honestly expressing how he feels about suffering and abuse. Slowly read the words out loud. Read as much or as little as you want. See if you can relate to either of these passages. Then, write down your own reaction or complaint to the Lord.

Perhaps you don't even need passages like these to help you say what is on your heart. It might be so close to the surface that you are ready to spill it out. So, just do it. You might just whisper it to the Lord. Or, maybe you want to shout it. Some people use art—drawing or painting to express what is deep inside.

This time alone is not about you following any rules. It's not a test that you must complete correctly. This is a time for you to talk to God about your sexual abuse. It's a private conversation between the two of you, and however it happens is fine. Just say it like it is. Be honest, be real, and lay your feelings and every question down before the Lord. Ask Him to protect you and to help you to hear only His voice as you pray and listen.

If you're choosing to write but don't have any idea of how to begin, you may find it helpful to practice freewriting to start your dialogue with the Lord. To do this, first set a timer for ten minutes and start to write. The key is to keep writing until the timer rings. Don't quit. Just write and write and write—no matter what—without stopping.

During the allotted time, if you can't think of anything to write, simply put, "I don't know what to write, I don't know what to write" down on the paper. If you do this, thoughts should begin to flow again. Don't worry about spelling or grammar or "doing it right." God knows what you mean even if the words are not spelled correctly. This is not a school assignment, and it won't be graded. In fact, if you don't want to risk others reading your private words, you can simply plan to destroy the pages after you've finished.

Freewriting is a way to access that which is down deep inside of us. Our words become a stream into which our feelings and memories flow so that they can rise to the surface of our consciousness. This is what honest praying looks and sounds like. It is simply a heart laid open before God.

If you are still struggling with how to get started, you may find it helpful to use the following sentences as a way to begin forming your own questions.

❖ Lord, why didn't You stop _____ from abusing me?

❖ Where were You? What were You doing when I was being abused?

❖ Were You punishing me for something I did wrong?

❖ I cried out to You. Why didn't You answer?

❖ How can You let such evil happen?

❖ You didn't protect me. Is it because You don't love me?

Once you've asked your question, it's time to sit still and listen. You may sit for quite a while, or thoughts and answers may seem to flow down from heaven.

Pay special attention to impressions that you may receive. This might be a picture in your mind, a word, a saying, or a memory. Trust this as a response from the Lord and record it. Follow where that impression takes you. Hearing God's voice is supernatural and requires a faith-filled surrender that basically says, "I've asked. I believe You heard me and will answer."

The Lord may direct your mind to other verses in the Bible. If this happens, follow the nudge and look up those verses. Then, read each verse slowly. Ask the Lord to speak to you and to show you how the Scripture relates to you and your experience.

If angry feelings arise, tell that to the Lord. "I'm so mad!" It isn't unholy or disrespectful to talk this way to the Lord. He can handle all of our questions. The thing He warns against is hypocrisy. The basic meaning is "to pretend."[11]

We are in danger of being hypocritical when we have deep doubts and nagging questions but hide behind a mask that says, "Everything is okay. I know God loves me. My past doesn't affect me."

After you've said all you have to say, it's time to pay attention and listen for God to speak. Your part is to be still and to quiet your mind. Just sit and concentrate on listening. Ask God to open your spiritual eyes and ears so you can hear His voice.

Another thing to be aware of is that once God has your attention, He may begin to speak to you in many ways. After you leave this specific time of prayer, He may speak to your heart through a song or a comment you overhear at the grocery store.

Maybe you'll hear God speaking through some one close to you or in an article you read. Pay attention. Your questions have been offered up. Now, look around, be attentive, and hear what the Lord God Almighty has to say.

One survivor told me about a time when she was on a plane and in a lot of emotional pain. She didn't consider herself a Christian, but she was hurting so much that she said a silent prayer. "Lord, if You're real and if You care, I would really feel better if I had a cookie."

This may sound crazy to you, but she was just being honest with the Lord. She then got up from her seat and made her way down the aisle to the back of the plane to use the restroom. When she finished and opened the door, a flight attendant was standing right there. He handed her two packages of cookies, saying, "Here, these are for you. Take them."She took them and returned to her seat, knowing that God had heard her and that He really did care about her pain.

Now, let's go back to a question that may have come to you when you read about Hannah and how the Bible says that "the LORD had given her no children" (1 Samuel 1:5).

First, let's consider the impact that truth had on Hannah's personal life. She could do nothing to change her situation. It was beyond her control. She couldn't make it happen. I bet she had really tried to get pregnant, but she couldn't make her body do what she wanted.

Maybe you share this same struggle. You know the heartache of infertility. You may even link your inability to get pregnant to your sexual abuse. This was true for a survivor I know. She eventually was able to have children, but it was a long and difficult road.

Here is the point—this type of situation can lead us to acknowledge a foundational truth that some things are beyond our control. Acknowledging our own inability provides us with the opportunity to be open to and ask for God's supernatural power.

Hannah's anguish was so great that the only place she could go was to God. She knew He was her only hope. She went and cried out and gave it all to Him. Although it was her pain that compelled her to go to God, it was where she needed to be to find answers.

The questions remain: Why would God do this? Why would He make Hannah infertile? It caused her such sorrow. Her deep longing was denied, and the fact that she couldn't have children resulted in such harsh ridicule and verbal abuse from Peninnah.

Well, God's ways are higher than ours. Even though I can't say why He allowed Hannah to suffer like this, I do see the good that resulted from her sorrow. Her suffering caused her to go to God and cry out in prayer. She felt so distressed about not having children that she made a vow to give her firstborn back to God as a special servant.

The rest of the story is that the Lord did respond to Hannah's desperate prayer. He gave her a son in response to her prayer, and she dedicated that boy to the Lord. He became a mighty man of God—the prophet Samuel—who was vital in leading his nation in the ways of the Lord.

Please consider this. Hannah's deep desire and need led her to seek the Lord. In the same way, our hurts often propel us to seek God's help.If the Lord had given Hannah babies right away, like she wanted, do you think she would have ever considered dedicating her firstborn to the Lord's service?

Also, in 1 Samuel 1:20 we read, "and in due time she gave birth to a son. She named him Samuel, for she said, 'I asked the LORD for him.'" Her temporary suffering caused her to go to God, and that resulted in great good for many people because her son became a mighty man of God.

Not only did the Lord bless Hannah with Samuel, He blessed her with other children as well. First Samuel 2:21 records, "And the LORD gave Hannah three sons and two daughters. Meanwhile, Samuel grew up in the presence of the LORD."

In Hannah's story we see that God responded when she cried out to Him from an honest heart. He will do the same for you. "The LORD is close to the brokenhearted; he rescues those whose spirits are crushed" (Psalm 34:18).

Hard times and sorrow can be agents of change if we take time to consider God and His plan. Suffering can offer us insight and lead us away from selfishness. We can choose how we will respond to the circumstances we face. The Lord promises to use suffering for our good.

One survivor I know works with children. She is very tender and loving and tries hard to show each child that they are special and valuable. She does this in part because she never felt protected or cherished as a child.

Of course, it would have been better if she had never been sexually abused and if she had parents who treated her well. But our world is full of evildoers and sin. How will we respond to this fact? Will we add to it by being bitter, angry, hateful, and mean? Or, will we attempt to make the world a better place for others?

In our pain, if we look to the Lord, He will take the sorrow and suffering we endured and use it for good. This is a marvelous miracle of love. Even this book is a small example of God working in this way. I would never have written a book on this topic if I had not been sexually abused and, as a result, faced obstacles in my marriage. God has used it for good.

So, would it have been better for God to have spared me that trauma? Or, is it better for other survivors to benefit from these words which are written out of my own experience? I am here to say that I would not change a thing about the way God has directed my life. The pain was worth it if I can help someone else to find the healing that Jesus is offering—the healing that He alone can give.

*Chapter* **9**

# Double Life

## Ms. Tanner's Story

"Thanks for your help, Ms. Tanner. Spanish is my favorite subject because of you."

I smiled at the pert sophomore. "And students who really care about learning make teaching the best job in the world."

She slung her backpack over her shoulder and walked toward the door.

"Have a great weekend," I called after her. *You can be sure I will.*

I gathered my belongings and headed to my car, waving to other teachers and students as I went. Then I saw, Ted Hall, one of our PE teachers. The sight of him filled me with shame as hot as fire. I ducked my head and quickly turned to walk the other way. *I wonder if he's told anyone?*

It took less than a year of teaching high school to know I'd found my niche and never wanted to do anything else. But at times, I feared that the life I led outside of my classroom might jeopardize my profession.

*What would people think if they knew the truth?* Most viewed me as a young professional with a successful life. I appeared to be a woman in control when, in fact, my life was spinning out of control. Seeing Ted reminded me of that.

Just last week, my two girlfriends had joined me at a local bar . . . "That one," I whispered to Trisha and Nancy, lifting my chin toward the tall man with the broad shoulders and thin mustache.

Their snickers told me that being my bar buddies for nearly a year had convinced them that I never failed to get my man. I picked them, used them, and moved on. I raised my eyebrows in preparation.

Trisha gave me the thumbs up sign and Nancy said, "Go for it."

I flashed a smiled before turning away from the two women who shared this part of my life. Pulling my green, clingy T-shirt down over my tight fitting jeans and curved hips, I slowly approached him from behind.

Leaning in, I caught his attention and held his gaze with my deep blue eyes. "How ya doing?"

His eyes met mine briefly before sweeping over my body, pausing in all the significant places. He used his tongue to play with his mustache while his eyes roamed. I wondered if he was a good kisser.

His eyes locked with mine and he smiled. "Doing great, now that you showed up." He inched forward on the bar stool and I tipped my head nearer to his. I touched his arm.

He took my hand. "Want to dance?"

"To start with," I said.

He stepped toward me and whispered, "Then, what?"

I tossed my head. "Some dancing, some dinner, some drinks—and some time alone." I gave him a look that told him I wanted him.

He gulped and led me to the dance floor.

As he did, I glanced at my friends and winked. They nodded in admiration. I felt a rush of excitement. *I love this part.* I began to move purposefully to the music, losing myself in the game of seduction.

Years had shown me that the men and women who looked for sex come from every imaginable background. Yet deep down, I also sensed that people who did what I did and slept with nearly one hundred strangers a year, had a history—a past defined by abuse. Mine was all-inclusive—severe physical beatings complete with screaming tirades and emotional torture. And, of course, let's not forget the sexual exploitation.

As a child, I worked hard trying to please my parents, wanting desperately to earn their love and acceptance. For years I made attempts to analyze and avoid what might detonate their rage only to discover that there was no logical pattern to their seething violence.

"You stupid little tramp," my mother screamed. "Where'd you put my lipstick?"

"I didn't touch it, Mommy." I backed away. "Really—I don't know where it is."

My tears acted like fuel. Her anger exploded. She swung her purse, smacking the side of my face. The buckle split my lip. "Shut up, Liar."

I shut up, hoping that she'd simmer down and find something else to do. That way I could get some ice for my mouth and finish getting ready for school.

That day I spent a lot of time thinking about what I'd done to deserve her wrath. It never occurred to me that fury might simply reside inside both my parents.

I never considered that they might be angry or deeply disappointed at life, or that I wasn't really the cause of the rage inside them. I only knew that constant violence defined our family; most often I was the recipient.

In order to survive, I quickly learned to play the pretend game. As soon as I walked out my front door, I became the perfect girl from the ideal family. Through the years, I earned academic awards, won prizes for my high school track team, and tried to convince myself that if I did everything correctly, my life would straighten out. Then the big, gaping hole in my heart would disappear. It never did. Still I played the game, living two lives—one acceptable and the other one hidden and driven by unmet needs and passions.

My search to be filled cost me searing pain when, as a young teen, one GI after another on the military base where I lived discarded me after our sexual encounters.

At age thirteen, I met Chuck, a strong GI with dark eyes and skin. He won my heart as well as my body when he brought me chocolates.

As I ate them, he'd kiss my ear and whisper, "You're the most beautiful woman I've ever seen."

He even talked to me and asked my opinion about things. His touch was tender when he gave me back rubs. Chuck was the first person to ever tell me, "I love you."

I believed him with all my heart and soul and imagined riding away with him in his red pickup truck. I'd use the small grey suitcase from under my parent's bed to take a few things with me. Then Chuck would take me far from my twisted life and we'd have a happy little family.

But he was wrong about me being a woman. Or maybe flattery was just a device he used along with the candy and tender touches to get what he wanted. I was still a child and he a grown man who was not foolish enough to let anyone know what he did with a minor in private. When his new orders came, he left without me. A note, taped to the top of a box of chocolates, said, "Thanks for the good times."

I ran into the woods behind the school gymnasium and wept, rocking back and forth, clutching that stupid red heart-shaped box.

*There must be something wrong with me.* I tried to figure out why I couldn't convince anyone to love me. *I'm just not worth loving.* Rejection as heavy as a mountain crushed me. Its weight destroyed all my remaining little girl dreams. *But I loved him! I gave him everything.*

I opened the box and stuffed a handful of chocolates into my mouth, nearly gagging as I chewed and sobbed.

*Chuck said he loved me.* I groaned. *Why didn't he take me with him?* Fresh pain tore at my fragile self-image. *It's because he didn't want me . . .*

I cried until there was nothing left. Then, empty and numb, I sat motionless except for the shiver that came when a cloud passed in front of the sun.

Slowly, things inside me began to shift. Into that barren place an ugly and cruel determination rose. *I don't care what it takes; I will never, ever be hurt like that again.*

Looking down at the half eaten box of chocolates, I chose an oval one with dark sprinkles. My mouth started to water as I lifted it to inhale the deep, rich scent. Holding the chosen morsel between my thumb and two fingers, I slowly examined its perfect shape that was covered with a lovely silky brown chocolate layer. I squeezed, watching as pink raspberry cream oozed out of the crushed sides. Sliding it onto my tongue, I sucked my fingers clean before clamping my teeth deep into the smashed candy. I'll never forget the way it coated the inside of my mouth with a smooth, sweet taste that left me desperate for more.

From that day on, I sought relief the only way I knew. I gave men what they needed to get the attention I craved. Back then, I thought the pain of Chuck's betrayal would never leave me. But in time, it left—just like him. I can still taste chocolate with raspberry when I remember.

After a while, a new hope stirred. I convinced myself that I just needed to find the right man—a good man who would really love me enough. I am still searching relentlessly, week-after-week, year-after-year, bed-after-bed. There is no such man; at least, I haven't found him. Maybe one day I will.

Before I even graduated from high school, I vowed to never let another man use my body. Instead, I determined that I would be the one to use my body to control them. In the process, during sexual release the gaping wound in my heart was soothed. I felt satisfied, for an instant, until it turned to self-disgust.

During my adult years, I knew when the comfort had given way to humiliation. That's when I'd snarl at my conquest, "Get up. Leave. I'm done with you."

Then I'd stare at the ceiling. *What's wrong with me? No one will ever want to marry me once they know what I've done. Why do I do this over and over?*

But even in that moment of remorse I would begin to make plans for the next time when I could subdue my pain by controlling a man.

## Relating to the Story

* Are you able to identify with the woman in this story?

* Would you describe yourself as an integrated, authentic person?

* Is the person you are inside the same person you let others see?

* How do you feel about this woman and the way she lives?

Understand it-------------Don't blame her--------------It's awful

We all have passions, needs, desires, urges, and cravings. These are a powerful part of being human that add beauty or bring bondage to our lives. From the list below, which would you guess are Ms. Tanner's strongest longings?

| Wants to be loved | Longs to be valued | Wants to feel special |
|---|---|---|
| Desires intimacy | Feels lonely | Needs security |
| Seeks relationships | Has sexual needs | Empty inside |

## *Recognizing the Issues ~ Fill the Holes*

There isn't one item in this list that is wrong. We were created to experience love, intimacy, and affection. We want to matter to someone and want our lives to have significance. These are real needs, and it is natural for us to seek to have them met. When channeled in healthy ways, such passions provide us with positive motivation that can bring joyful benefits. But, if we allow our urges to direct our choices, we can find ourselves dominated by self-destructive addictions.

Think of these human passions as a fire in a fireplace. When contained, fire gives light and provides warmth; it is a very positive force. But unattended flames that are allowed to burn freely can be whipped by the wind and become uncontrollable and destructive. Is there a way to channel our passions so that they bring life to others and to ourselves?

Let's talk about human longings. Each person is created with a void in his or her spirit that can only be filled with the Lord God. This empty spot is God's tailor-made dwelling place. Until we welcome Him into our lives, we feel restless, unsettled, and incomplete. We long to have this spot filled and sense that we are supposed to be whole. Some of us have been keenly aware of our spiritual yearnings since childhood. Others have ignored or denied them for so long that we have trouble identifying any type of spiritual hunger or consciousness.

The Lord created us with this longing on purpose so that our desire to be complete would lead us into His loving arms. When we respond to God's invitation and He comes to dwell in us, He takes up residence in His prepared place in our hearts and fills our emptiness. He is the fullness we seek. So, this God-shaped vacuum, and the yearning it creates, is a gift to us. It reminds us we are created for God and that He adores us and wants to be a part of our lives.

Spiritual desire resonates that we are more than dust—more than intellect, intent, and emotions. We are a living soul with a spirit and a body. As C. S. Lewis said, "If we find ourselves with a desire that nothing in this world can satisfy, the most probable explanation is that we were made for another world."

It is from this empty place that holy longings arise. Our deep spiritual desire is actually a yearning to be closely, eternally connected with the One who made us; to receive His unfathomable love for us; and to love Him with our total selves. It is our most basic need. And the Lord patiently pursues us, not in a frightening, selfish way, but with gentle wooing. Consider some of the ways our God draws us.

✤ He takes care of us. He is the provider of the air we breathe and the water we drink. He designed the plants that we eat for nourishment. He planned for the sun to be situated far enough away so that its heat does not consume us but is close enough that we benefit from its light and warmth.

✤ He gives us gifts. Beautiful skies, sunsets, waves that sing the song of the seas as they meet sandy beaches. A baby's soft cheek, the sound of thunder, colors of spring, the sound of laughter.

✤ He doesn't give up on us. From childhood we are conscious of the empty place, and that awareness never really leaves us until we are filled with Jesus. It tugs us toward Him when we are making a harmful choice. We hear its call in beautiful music that sweeps in and through us. We acknowledge His presence when we feel remorse for our wrong actions because we know that we were created for better things.

❖ He shows us the truth about the world. Sometimes it is a powerful story that resonates genuineness, or an undeserved kindness. When we hear or read the Bible, our heart leaps with hope. Words in a song, on a talk show, overheard in the grocery store, or spoken by a child can reveal truth to us.

❖ He hears and answers us. Prayer is God's way of saying, "Let's talk." We can bring our concerns to Him and He'll give us guidance. Sharing our joys and sorrows with Him reminds us that we are never alone. We ask for help and He'll direct us. We pray for others and He hears.

Enjoying a vital, living relationship with God is central to everything else. Total healing begins at this point. When we're connected to the Lord, our relationship becomes a wellspring that overflows into every other area of life. Jesus compares our spiritual craving to being thirsty and promises to personally quench our thirst. Read His words found in John 4:14: "Those who drink the water I give will never be thirsty again. It becomes a fresh, bubbling spring within them, giving them eternal life."

One way to think about this God-given void is to compare it to a missing puzzle piece. Until this central piece is put in its proper place, the puzzle remains unfinished and incomplete. But when it is found and placed where it belongs, every other piece is unified and the entire picture is complete. All together, the connected pieces of our lives reveal the beauty and meaning intended by the Creator.

While the missing puzzle piece is a God-given gift intended to lead us to find our satisfaction in Him, we also have other empty places in our souls that have not been created by God.

These most often come from other people. When those who are supposed to take care of us fail to meet our basic needs for security, love, acceptance, approval, and protection, we are deeply injured. They withheld what we needed. Sometimes these were the same people who purposefully inflicted pain.

Early in life, these types of wounds often come through others. But it doesn't take us long to begin to make our own hurtful, willful, and poor choices that cause damage to our souls. Demanding our own way, even when it isn't safe or good for us, is actually natural to our sinful nature. No one has to teach us to say "no" and "I can do it myself."

Think of these types of injuries as holes in our soul. A hole is nothing but an empty place. Emptiness inside doesn't feel right. It bothers us, and we don't like it.

As we go through life, we deepen the holes in our souls by dwelling on them. When we remember the scenarios that caused the initial pain and replay the details of the event, the pain deepens.

Making poor choices and going against God's ways also expands the holes in our souls. If our soul wounds are not healed, they intensify. As time goes on, it's harder to ignore the pain they cause.

We begin to throw things, anything and everything, into the holes in our soul so we won't feel empty. Where do we run? To food, drink, sex, porn, romance books, fame, work, money, shopping, gambling, chocolate, sleep, drugs, self-harm, rage, blaming, gossip, or fantasy?

You may have a different place where you go for comfort. Each one is an idol. An idol is anything we turn to in an attempt to meet our needs instead of turning to God.

There is a distinction between the emptiness of a wounded soul and the missing puzzle piece. Both feel like a

lack, both cause us to seek completion, and both kindle desires and longings because being empty is an ache that we
can't ignore. We want to find a way to make the pain go away.

❖ What would you guess is the primary source of Ms.
Tanner's longings?

Missing puzzle piece----------------------------------Wounded soul

❖ How is Ms. Tanner attempting to fill up the empty
places within her?

Confusion comes and addictions can form when we
mistakenly try to fill up our emptiness from the wrong
direction. When we work from the outside in, thinking that
by filling the holes in our soul we will also satisfy our deep
spiritual hunger, we are mistaken. The only way to be truly
filled is to begin on the inside and move out.

We become spiritually whole when we find the missing
puzzle piece which represents union with God Almighty
through Jesus Christ. The overflow of this relationship begins
to fill the holes in our soul. Jesus promised this when He said,
"'Let anyone who is thirsty come to me and drink. Whoever
believes in me, as Scripture has said, rivers of living water will
flow from within them.' By this he meant the Spirit, whom
those who believed in him were later to receive. Up to that
time the Spirit had not been given, since Jesus had not yet
been glorified" (John 7:37-39 NIV).

Do you see that Jesus is revealing the direction in which
transformation travels? First, our deepest spiritual needs,
those within our inmost heart, are filled by Jesus. Then, His
life flows out from there into our souls.

Earlier, when we compared human passions to fire, we asked, "Is there a way to channel our passions so that they bring life to others and to ourselves?" The answer is, "Yes!" When the power of God, through the Holy Spirit, flows from our innermost being to our soul, we are able to begin to exercise dominion over our natural desires.

Think about the story of Ms. Tanner and how devastated she felt as a young teen when Chuck abandoned her. The rejection left a huge hole in her soul. She also had the ache of the missing puzzle piece in her spirit. The combined emptiness seemed like too much to bear and so she began a pattern of acting out in destructive ways. But her empty places were never filled.

Her story would have turned out differently if she had gone to God in her pain. *Lord, please help me!* Whenever we confess our need for God, He draws near. The Lord would have responded to her and eased her sorrow. She would have become spiritually whole. From this place of strength she could have handled the ache of Chuck's rejection. Yes, it still would have hurt, but she would have been empowered to make wise choices about how to live her life despite that painful experience. It could have become a positive turning point for her.

As soon as God enters in, living waters flow out. The living water is the very Spirit of God. When He lives inside of us, we are changed and given the power to say no to unrighteousness and harmful behaviors.

While we can still sin and make poor choices, Christ's presence influences us toward life and gives us new desires. This is the process of transformation. It occurs over time as we learn to make choices based on pleasing the Lord. If Ms. Tanner had cried out to the Lord, He would have healed her wounds so the she could have responded out of her overflow instead of out of her lack.

A person may find the missing puzzle piece and be made whole in Jesus yet still be suffering from unhealed soul wounds. Or, there are survivors who were already spiritually filled when their abuse occurred. The injuries inflicted on their soul are just as grievous and maybe more so if the perpetrator claimed to be a Christian.

While knowing the love of Christ gives us comfort and hope, it will not prevent us from the pain caused by sins committed against us. Opening up our wounded souls to the life-giving water may come in stages and occur over a period of time, as we are ready. This is okay. Being spiritually complete gives us the courage to seek healing for our emotional injuries. Some, as we will see with the bleeding woman, receive immediate healing on every level when they open up to the love of Christ.

Please believe me, the Lord has special affection for you. He will not rest but will continue to invite you to come home to Him. His family is incomplete without you. There is a vacant picture frame on His wall, meant for you. He has a place in His heart that can only be filled by you.

I understand that the concept of a loving God who adores us is difficult for many survivors. In his book, *Passion for Jesus* (Lake Mary, FL: Charisma House, 2007), author Mike Bickle writes, "Our ideas about God—who He is and what He is like —come naturally through our relationships with earthly authority figures. When these are distorted, so are our ideas about God" (1). It takes great faith, the kind that our dear woman had, to trust that if you will only come to Jesus, He'll touch your life with healing.

The choice is ours. That's amazing. He is all-powerful, but He will not force Himself on anyone. He doesn't demand anything that we don't give freely. He beckons each soul with pure and tender love. We get to choose if we'll respond to His invitation or utterly reject Him. He is after our freely given surrender because He truly loves us and will never, ever stop loving us. Until we find our fulfillment in Jesus, our longings, desires, and passions will not be satisfied.

It's obvious that many people do not seek satisfaction from the Lord. Even those who find Jesus to be their primary source of life and joy may go elsewhere at times. This might stem from patterns learned growing up or acquired in order to survive. It also comes when we continue to indulge in activities that we enjoy but that are not truly beneficial.[12]

Now, let's address ways in which we may have reacted as a result of being sexually abused. Once we have them named, we can try to determine ways in which we may react.

As a survivor, can you identify any of the emotions, attitudes, or beliefs listed below as true for you?

| I feel ashamed | I'm worthless | No one loves me |
|---|---|---|
| I'm unworthy | I pretend I'm okay | I have a secret life |
| I'm angry | I'm stupid | I'm unwanted |
| I can't be fixed | I hate myself | I'm to blame |
| I'm no good | I'm ugly and dirty | No one wants me |
| No one likes me | I'm a disappointment | I'm a failure |
| I'm empty inside | I can't be forgiven | I have no future |

My heart grieved as I wrote those words and thought about survivors who struggle with such negative perceptions of themselves. We come to false conclusions about ourselves through the things we experience. If another person used us, discarded us, devalued us, betrayed us, lied to us, tormented us, or refused to protect us, that is sure to influence the way we view our world and the way we see ourselves.

It's only when we allow Jesus to fill us up on the inside and let His life flow out over our wounded souls that we start to heal.

- ❖ Into the hole of unlovable, the Lord says, "I have loved you, my people, with an everlasting love. With unfailing love I have drawn you to myself" (Jeremiah 31:3).

- ❖ Into feelings of deep rejection, He says, "The LORD will not reject his people; he will not abandon his special possession" (Psalm 94:14).

- ❖ To that place of "I have so much pain!" He assures us with these words: "But you belong to God, my dear children. You have already won a victory over those people, because the Spirit who lives in you is greater than the spirit who lives in the world" (1 John 4:4).

## Requesting God's Help

"Oh Lord, You know how much I want to believe that You love me, that You think I am special. You know my struggles and what things I turn to instead of You. My holes are so deep I feel like they may swallow me. Please help me get out of this pit. Forgive me, Lord. You are holy and I am sinful. Please, Jesus, reveal Yourself to me. Amen."

## Reflecting on Scripture

### Mark 5:25-32

[25] A woman in the crowd had suffered for twelve years with constant bleeding.

[26] She had suffered a great deal from many doctors, and over the years she had spent everything she had to pay them, but she had gotten no better. In fact, she had gotten worse.

[27] She had heard about Jesus, so she came up behind him through the crowd and touched his robe.

[28] For she thought to herself, "If I can just touch his robe, I will be healed."

[29] Immediately the bleeding stopped, and she could feel in her body that she had been healed of her terrible condition.

[30] Jesus realized at once that healing power had gone out from him, so he turned around in the crowd and asked, "Who touched my robe?"

[31] His disciples said to him, "Look at this crowd pressing around you. How can you ask, 'Who touched me?'"

[32] **But he kept on looking around to see who had done it.**

Have you ever experienced being in a crowded place but only focusing on one person? Or, have you ever known what it feels like to have someone only have eyes for you—to single you out in a group and to give you that special look?

This verse reminds me of that. It reflects a personal, persistent pursuing. Jesus kept on looking for the one specific person whose faith had released God's power.

He was looking for her. Even though there were multitudes interested in Him who would have welcomed His personal attention, at that moment Jesus was only interested in finding our precious sister.

I know it's a bit of a holdover from Cinderella, yet doesn't the female heart long to be wanted and hope to be pursued? Not pursued in a frightening way, for selfish ends, but pursued because we're desired and chosen. Ephesians 1:4 says, "Even before he made the world, God loved us and chose us in Christ to be holy and without fault in his eyes." Isn't that wonderful? He loves you. You are chosen!

## Responding to God's Word

Do you think our dear woman knew that Jesus was looking for her? Do you know that He is looking for you? The fact that Jesus took the time to seek her reflects the part of God's character that corresponds to our need to be valued.

Since each of us is created in God's likeness, any good quality we possess somehow reflects His nature. If we express kindness, it's not because kindness originates with us, but rather it stems from the fact that the One who fashioned us is kind.

So when we long to be loved, it is because God first loved us and longs for us. When we long to be noticed, it is because God notices us. We see this by the way Jesus acts. He demonstrates His persistent desire for each one of us. He is relentless in His pursuit.

In this true account, Jesus kept on seeking out a single person even though those around Him were urging him to move on. This is true love. This is Jesus. He will not rest until we respond to Him.

When I use the word *desire* to describe God's interest in us, I hope you are not offended. His passion toward you is pure, not selfish. His true love seeks your best and longs to bring you blessing, comfort, and security.

Those who have experienced the perversion of sexual abuse may struggle with linking human sexuality to a good and wise Creator. But the truth remains that God's design for human sexuality is very good. It has been twisted and distorted in the most horrendous ways by the lusts of sinful people, but that is not what God intended.

Recovering a godly perspective about sex is a foundational part of our healing. Picture it this way. The Bible says that God formed the woman, Eve. The basic meaning of the word formed is "to fashion." So our loving God carefully shapes female sexuality into a lovely body, much like a skilled sculptor might form a graceful vase.

But what if someone uses a hammer on that vase and shatters it? The original form is destroyed. All the pieces are there, but if they were glued back together, the vase would leak and not function as originally designed.

The way God remakes our sexual identity is more like the dedicated potter who gathers the bits and pieces of our broken lives into His trustworthy hands, wets them with His tears, and reshapes the clay into a new and beautiful creation.

He remakes us, showing us His intent and shaping our hearts and minds to receive a new understanding of our sexuality and how it is an integral and blessed part of being female.

Part of this process is accepting that we long to be pursued and that the Lord is the One who seeks us in righteousness. He is the true Lover of our souls who will never give up on us. He woos us, calls us, and expresses His love in letters (the Bible) and in gifts (like waterfalls and cherries). In the afternoon thunderstorm He declares that His heart beats for us alone. His attentions are overwhelming and His love for us is unending.

When we take a tiny step toward trusting Him, like the woman who bled did, and when we reach out our hand because we believe He will heal us, He will. He is the Eternal One who stops and takes notice of each one of us. He will stand still, look around, and wait until we respond and come to Him.

Jesus searched for the one who had touched His robe. Though He certainly knew exactly who she was, He stood there and waited. He gave her time to come to Him. He waited. And right this very moment, Jesus is looking for you. He is waiting for you to step out of the crowd. Maybe no one in your family is a Christ-follower. Maybe they all claimed to be but still you were wounded.

Are you one who has always hidden from God in a crowd of people or zealous activity? Perhaps you have excelled in a career or been a supermom. Have you hidden under extra weight or a hot temper? He is calling you to Himself.

What ways do you employ to try to keep your distance from the One who made you? Whatever the means, He is more patient.

He will never give up on you. You matter that much to Him. He wants you to be His very own beloved one. He wants all of your love—the love of your heart, your mind, your soul, and your strength.

When you give your whole self to Him, He fills up every empty place. If you have never responded to the compelling offer of Jesus, the time is now. The prayer is simple.

## Releasing It All to the Lord

"Lord Jesus, if You really do love me, please show me. Are You seeking me out? Do you want me to come to You? Are You waiting for me? I come to You now. I have nothing to offer but my need, my broken heart, my pain, my disappointment, and my sorrow. I can't survive without Your help, so here I am. Please take my life. I surrender to You now. Amen."

*Chapter 10*

# I Have to Do Something!

## Patty's Story

Driving through an unfamiliar city late at night, I took a wrong turn. *Lord, please help me to find my hotel.* After a long day of delayed flights and lost luggage, I dreaded my early morning business meeting without a good night's sleep.

*Thank You, Lord, for getting me here safely. I don't see how this inconvenience could be for good, except to help me learn more patience, but I'm choosing to thank You for arranging my day according to Your will.*

Even though the battery on my phone was low, I decided to use it to find my bearings. Pulling into the parking lot of a 7-11, I checked to be sure the car doors were locked before turning off the engine, and switched on my phone. As I waited for the map to load, I glanced out the front window.

A chill ran up my spine. An older man with "#1 Dad" printed on his T-shirt, gripped the hand of a young girl. Even though it was warm outside, the girl wore a sweatshirt with the hood pulled low and tight around her face. Her features were obscured and strands of straggly blond hair stuck out from under the edge of the hood. She stared at the ground. Her red sweatpants were too short, and her yellow flip-flops too big.

I had to do something! I lifted my phone and snapped a picture. The unkempt man led the child across the parking lot toward a white pickup truck. My heart leapt to my throat and a familiar terror gripped me as he opened the door and put her into the truck . . . Suddenly I was eight years old again climbing into a white car as a man held the door open for me.

Refusing to let the memory invade the moment, I quickly dialed 9-1-1. Then, I pulled out to follow the pickup down the street. I know it isn't safe to use a cell phone when driving, but it's even more risky to suspect abuse and not report it.

So, I kept a distance behind the truck while I told the 9-1-1 operator, "I think I just spotted an abducted child."

I explained the situation and answered all of the operator's questions. Before long, a police car pulled in front of me. The officer gave me a nod as he passed, indicating he would handle things from here.

*I can't just leave her.* I kept following. *I won't get in the way.* I slowed but still had a clear view since the streets were nearly deserted this late on a weeknight.

Two more cruisers turned from side streets. *They must have run his plates and have something, or why would there be so many?*

My heart sped up, but I didn't allow my foot to press harder on the accelerator. *I don't want to interfere with her rescue.* "Please, Lord, help her. Help them set her free!"

The scene suddenly exploded into activity, with flashing lights and wailing sirens. The pickup shot away at high speed, and that's when I knew for certain that I'd done the right thing.

I prayed out loud, pleading, *Please, don't let him hurt her! Let her live. Rescue her, Jesus, just like You rescued me.*

Once I caught up to the scene, I parked at the curb across the street and watched. The unkempt man now wore handcuffs. A police officer forced him into the back of one of the vehicles.

Nearby, a grandfatherly officer squatted in front of the child. He slowly untied the string of her sweatshirt and folded back the hood. The little girl looked both scared and relieved, and for some reason she looked vaguely familiar. Everything in me wanted to rush to her, to gather her up and console her.

*She needs comfort! She needs me to hold her.* But I knew that in this pivotal moment, my interfering would only cause confusion. *She doesn't need that. She's suffered enough.*

The child pointed toward the police car where her perpetrator had been taken and fear clouded her young face. The officer near her glanced to where she pointed and turned back to her. He seemed to be telling her something. Whatever he said changed her expression from terrified to peaceful. Suddenly, she threw her arms around his neck and clung to him, sobbing.

Relief as welcome as a long awaited rain, flooded me. I blinked away tears as the officer lifted the little girl, and carried her to another waiting police car. *She's safe. Thank You, God, that she's safe.* Even as I gave thanks, troubling emotions began to bubble up inside me.

I told myself, *It's okay. He's a good man. He's helping her.*

Still, I couldn't control the feelings that overtook me as for the second time that night I watched a man putting that little girl into a car. I fought the memory. *No! Don't go there.* As hard as I tried, the sight unwillingly took me back to that day over twenty years ago.

~ ~ ~ ~ ~

What a perfect spring morning to ride my bike to my grandparent's house just a few blocks from where I lived. Granddad said I could help him paint the back steps, and Grammy needed my help baking oatmeal raisin cookies. Granddad ate two cookies every morning right after he finished breakfast. "They keep my mind sharp," he said.

I still remembered the song I sang when the white car slowed. "Twinkle, twinkle little star, how I wonder what you are."

The man in the car called out to me. "Excuse me."

"Yes?"

"What's your name?"

"Patty."

"Then you're the one I'm looking for," he said. "Your mother sent me. She said to look for a little girl named Patty riding a pink bike on Alpine Street."

I stopped peddling. "My mother sent you?"

"Yes. She asked me to come and find you. She needs help right away. There's been an accident."

I jumped off my bike. "What happened?" I started to cry.

He stopped the car and got out. "Don't worry." He took me by the shoulders. "I told her I'd find you and drive you straight home."

"Thank you," I said as he opened the back door and I slid into his car.

We drove off. I didn't see my family again until he was done with me. Later, I learned that the ordeal that seemed as if it would never end actually lasted only five days. I was one of the lucky ones. I don't know why Uncle B, as he called himself, let me live. He dropped me off within walking distance of a deserted campground located about a day's drive from my home.

The horror of his assaults still gripped me at unexpected moments. I fought the images that flashed through my mind, causing my body to react. Although my family knew I'd been kidnapped, they never could have imagined the particulars of what I'd endured.

I never talked about the details, and no one but the police ever asked. And I told them very little. It was too shameful to speak of the things he did to me and made me do to him. No, I kept those evil secrets hidden. Each one was mine to bear; I refused to put that burden on anyone else.

Long before I found the park ranger, Uncle B had fled. He had been extremely precise in the planning and execution of his crime and got away without being caught. Knowing that he might still be out there somewhere, looking for another child to use for his perverted pleasure, caused me the most agony.

A tap on my car window brought me to the present. I blinked and saw the officer who first passed me standing by my car.

I rolled down the window. "Yes?"

"Hello, ma'am. Are you the one who called 9-1-1?"

"Yes, I called about an abducted child."

He offered his hand. "I'm Officer Bell."

"I'm Patty." I gave him a weak smile and shook his hand. "I can't tell you how relieved I am that you caught the guy—and rescued that little girl."

"You played a vital role in what happened here tonight."

I felt myself blush.

"Still," Officer Bell said, "it wasn't safe for you to follow us and then to park like this, so close by. What if there had been gunfire?" His voice was gruff but his expression kind.

"Yes, sir." I choked up and had to swallow my emotion. "I'm sorry. I just had to be sure she was safe."

He nodded. It seemed he understood. "Well, Patty, I need to verify all your information. You're an eyewitness and so we'll need you to make a statement."

"Will I have to testify in court?" A rush of heat swept through me—a mixture of vengeance and dread.

"That's a possibility." He took a few moments to record all of the pertinent information.

I slipped my driver's license back into my wallet. "Who was that man, the one who had the child?"

"Well, ma'am, I can tell you this. That kidnapper has outstanding warrants in three states. And the truck had been reported stolen."

That took my breath.

"It also looks like this might be the little girl abducted last week from Arizona."

"The one taken from the mall?"

He nodded. "Yes. Jessica Michelle Martin."

"Jessica?" *That's why she looked familiar.* "I saw her picture on TV!" An image of a smiling blue-eyed girl with long blond hair came to mind. "And I heard that interview with her family." Her brother said that he let her go to the bathroom and she never came back. His parents appeared desperate, and I thought about how my own family must have felt when I disappeared.

Officer Bell smiled. "Jessica's family will be overjoyed to have her home."

I nodded.

Officer Bell leaned in a bit. "Good endings like this keep me going." He paused to wipe his eyes with the back of his hand. "Thank you for caring enough to call. It's citizens like you who help us do our job to keep the innocent safe." With that he tapped the car roof and left.

I sat there, parked at the curb, for a long while, stunned as I recalled my reaction to the news reports of the young girl who had gone missing while at the mall with her older brother.

*I cried out to You, Lord! I asked You to please, please protect her and to rescue her and to return her to her family. You did it! You heard me and . . . You let me be a part of the answer.*

Tears came and I let them flow freely. *Oh, thank You. Thank You! Thank You for delayed flights and for lost luggage and for letting me get disoriented trying to find my hotel. And, Lord, thank You most of all for letting me see Jessica and allowing me to be the one to call for help.*

## Relating to the Story

* How can you relate to Patty's feeling that telling the details of her abuse might be a burden to others?

* If another person has ever trusted you enough to share a deep pain, how did that make you feel?

❖  How might others who have been wounded find comfort in hearing Patty talk about her experience and how
she has dealt with it?

❖  How did Patty's abduction as a child contribute to her
noticing the little girl and propel her to call 9-1-1?

❖  What was it that made Patty sensitive to the fact that
the little girl in this story might have been abducted?

❖  How might your experience qualify you to help others?

## Recognizing the Issues ~ Courage to Confess

Modern media makes it possible for us to be riveted to
news reports about a missing child. We share concern for the
child's safety and hope for her safe return.  But it's curious to
me that many of us are equally captivated by the dysfunction
of others. People's sinful choices are broadcast on TV screens
and reported in tabloids. Yet, we are often reluctant to
scrutinize our own lives. An exception to this might be those
raised in an environment that required intense self-scrutiny.
For most, however, recognizing our own sinfulness or ana-
lyzing our failings doesn't even occur to us. It certainly isn't a
natural instinct; however, hiding our faults and making
excuses for our weakness is easy.

We can trace this response back to the Garden of Eden
when, as soon as the first couple sinned, they covered up and
hid.

Like them, we have the same natural response to sin. We
try to hide it. Sometimes, it is our own sins. Other times, it's
the sins committed against us that we cover up. We really

don't want to be found out, and don't like the idea of talking about what's happened. This is the way we normally deal with our own or our family's sin. But it isn't the correct way. It feels right, but it isn't. It is actually the opposite of what we must do in order to be free from the power of sin.

Adam and Eve ran away and hid when they heard the sound of the Lord coming to take His daily walk with them. This is also how we often react when we feel shame or guilt. Our instinct is to run away and hide from God. Yet, in the garden, He called out, "Where are you?"

Of course the Lord God knew where the first couple were hiding. I think that His calling out, "Where are you?" was an invitation for them to come out from hiding—to tell the truth —to confess.

If we can just grasp the concept that as followers of Christ we are to live lives of confession, we would be less burdened with the weight of guilt and shame. Proverbs 28:13 says, "He who conceals his transgressions will not prosper, but he who confesses and forsakes them will find compassion" (NASB).

As we read on in the story of Adam and Eve, we see their response. After hiding, they began to blame others for their bad choices. Adam said it was Eve's fault, and she blamed the serpent. It is key for us to learn how to stop casting blame and to start taking responsibility. This may be difficult when our sinful choices have their root in our abuse, since our perpetrator is in fact guilty for that.

What about the sinful choices we make because we were abused? One survivor says that when she was first abused as a young girl, she was appalled. She knew it was wrong and didn't want any part of it.

Yet over time, as the abuse continued, it awakened in her a sexual awareness that developed into lust and unnatural desires. She actually hated and enjoyed the abusive encounters. This caused her to feel very conflicted and produced a load of guilt and shame which later compelled her into a sexual addiction.

In her healing journey, this survivor came to realize her own need to confess her sin of lust to the Lord. It's probably true that she would never have had to make such a confession if she'd never been sexually abused. However, when she confessed her own sin, it resulted in her being released from long standing feelings of shame and guilt. There's freedom in owning up to our own sins and asking God to take them away and forgive us.

For survivors, it's not usually our own sins that we find hardest to confess; it's the sins that were done to us. These also must be confessed. We need to tell the truth about sin— the sins committed against us and the sins we've committed against others.

This type of transparency seems terrifying. It makes us feel unsafe. But there is great power in telling the whole truth. Keeping the truth hidden in the dark doesn't work.

Another reason it can be hard for survivors to talk about their abuse is because of the threats they might have heard. Survivors are often burdened with *keeping the secret* of their sexual abuse. Maybe you were threatened that if you ever told, something terrible would happen to you or to someone you cared about.

As a child, one survivor was told by her uncle, "If you ever tell, I'll have to kill you." This made sense to her. And when she heard of a child murdered in the next county, she simply assumed, based on her own information, that her uncle must have done it because he had to.

Two other survivors I know had their pets slaughtered in front of them. A favorite dog was shot and the father said, "I brought you into this world, and I can take you out of it." A beloved goat had its throat slit. The survivor says, "I knew without a doubt that he could kill me just as easily."

Witnessing this type of cruelty as children convinces us that telling is unsafe. As adults, we need to come to terms with the terror that was instilled in us so long ago and recognize that talking about our abuse can actually release us from fear. Learning to think objectively about any threats that we heard and deciding to talk about our abuse will bring a new sense of power to our lives.

Truth is supposed to be proclaimed, and telling the truth sets us free. In the booklet, *Healing from Sexual Abuse*, Kathleen says, "It is vital for the victim to tell her story. Telling the story breaks the secrecy and shame . . . with anything fearful, the more you expose it to the light, the less power it holds" (15).

So telling the truth about your abuse is an important step to becoming well. Find one trusted person and tell them the whole truth of your story. This may be a trustworthy friend, sibling, or ministry leader. You may want to find a professional counselor as Kathleen did. She says, "A skillful professional counselor or a support group dealing with sexual abuse is critical to recovery" (15).

King David was a mighty leader, but he also sinned in very grievous ways. In Psalm 32:3 he addresses the consequences of his unconfessed sin. Although he's not talking about sins committed against him, his writing does reveal how keeping quiet about sin can have a physical effect.

"When I kept silent about my sin, my body wasted away through my groaning all day long" (NASB). He understood that things were bad in his life because he wasn't willing to talk about his sin. All hidden sin holds power—both the sins we commit and those sins committed against us.

## Requesting God's Help

"Lord, if it really is important for me to talk about my story, please make me willing. Show me when and who and what to say. Or, just help me to write it all down. Please show me the way that will work best for me to get it out into the open. I so much want to be better. Please heal me. Amen."

## Reflecting on Scripture

### Mark 5:25-33

> [25] A woman in the crowd had suffered for twelve years with constant bleeding.
> [26] She had suffered a great deal from many doctors, and over the years she had spent everything she had to pay them, but she had gotten no better. In fact, she had gotten worse.
> [27] She had heard about Jesus, so she came up behind him through the crowd and touched his robe.
> [28] For she thought to herself, "If I can just touch his robe, I will be healed."
> [29] Immediately the bleeding stopped, and she could feel in her body that she had been healed of her terrible condition.
> [30] Jesus realized at once that healing power had gone out from him, so he turned around in the crowd and asked, "Who touched my robe?"
> [31] His disciples said to him, "Look at this crowd pressing around you. How can you ask, 'Who touched me?'"
> [32] But he kept on looking around to see who had done it.

**³³ Then the frightened woman, trembling at the realization of what had happened to her, came and fell to her knees in front of him and told him what she had done.**

What word in this verse describes how this woman felt? We see that this precious woman is afraid. She is so frightened that she is trembling.

After all, coming up behind Jesus is one thing. In a crowd that size, touching His robe might not have seemed very risky. But having Him call out to ask her to identify herself— that must have been terrifying.

I'm sure it was incredible when Christ's healing power entered her body and her bleeding stopped. In my way of thinking, once that happened everything was accomplished. Her mission had been successful. It was time to go home.

But then, Jesus stopped. He turned around and asked, "Who touched me?"

It wasn't a general question. He asked a specific question. She must have known that He was speaking to her. Yet, she didn't answer immediately. She didn't rush forward with a raised hand, "Me! Me! I'm the one."

No, she waited.

So did Jesus.

She might have waited, hoping He'd give up on her and go on with the pressing matter of Jairus' dying daughter. She may have wished He wouldn't notice her, wouldn't single her out, and wouldn't make her confess.

"But he kept on looking around to see who had done it." He waited, and I think that as He waited, she knew He was waiting for her.

Our sweet sister had to make a choice. Would she respond to Jesus? He healed her. Since that's what she came for, why not just leave? Jesus was asking her to take another difficult step and identify herself. He wanted to talk to her, to relate to her face-to-face. Would she come, or would she ignore His request?

Each person ever born has this same choice to make. Christ calls out to each of us. We must decide if we will respond to Him or go on with our own plans. Often, in times of crisis, many will cry out to God. He responds to us. He draws near. He offers help, wisdom, and comfort. After He's acted on our behalf and the urgency subsides, what then?

Do we simply ignore what He's done for us and go on living as if He doesn't matter? Will our dear woman go back to her old life of isolation—to her life before she met Jesus— or will she take the next step and respond when He calls?

If she had gone back to her old life, if Jesus had not waited for her to identify herself, I think her healing would only have been physical.

Her bleeding would have stopped, but all of the other layers of her pain—being shunned and rejected, having her hopes dashed, suffering at the hands of those who were supposed to help her—these and more would have remained a part of who she was. She would have gone home better, but not totally healed.

Jesus cared for every aspect of this individual woman. He offered her the frightening opportunity of public confession. Throughout Scripture we see that confession is God's ordianed way for us to receive forgiveness, restoration, and peace.

So, Jesus is standing there waiting for her.

Look at how the New International Version records her response in Mark 5:33. (I have formatted it.)

Then
the woman,
knowing what had happened to her,
came
and fell at his feet and,
trembling with fear,
told him
the whole truth.

After Jesus stops, turns around, asks the question, and waits for her to reply, that's when our precious woman comes to Him.

Notice that she's still afraid, but still she comes. Fear doesn't stop her. What a woman of courage and faith. She is no longer sneaking up behind Him; now she is bowing low before Him. Her posture indicates that she recognizes Him as Lord of Lords. He is still surrounded by mobs of people. At this moment, I imagine those nearest to Him and the healed woman are watching silently and listening intently.

This is when our dear woman tells him the whole truth. This is public confession. We don't really know what she told Him, but the word "whole" means "any, ever, all." Perhaps she told Jesus that she had planned to sneak up, touch His robe, and slip away. Or maybe she confessed that she was unclean and had broken the law by even being there among so many people.

Maybe there was much more to tell. She would have confessed her own immoral behavior if that had caused her condition. She may have told Him about how others had falsely judged her or about how ashamed and guilty she felt. If sexual abuse caused her to bleed she would have told Jesus all about what happened to her. Whatever her story, she told it to Jesus. She told him everything.

## Responding to God's Word

Jesus came to take away our sins.[13] Confessing sin is like putting out the garbage can for Jesus to take it away. Isn't it amazing that He wants to do this? That He came to do this? That He is willing to do this? He took on every unspeakable offense so that we could be free from the bondage of sin.

So, dear one, I am challenging you to follow the example of this brave woman. Tell the whole truth. Tell your whole story, truthfully. First, tell it to Jesus. Write it as a prayer, or say it out loud. Then, find a trusted person and talk to him or her. Think carefully about the time and place. Prepare the person you've chosen for your confession by saying, "There's something very personal I'd like to share with you. Is that okay? It may take awhile. Would you like to come over to my house? I'll make coffee."

Another approach is to simply ask God to arrange the time, place, and person for your confession. This is what happened to this special woman. She had not planned on Jesus calling her. But when He did, she confessed, even though she was very afraid.

So when God brings the person, place, and time, do not hesitate. Take a deep breath and a huge step of faith and confess the whole truth.

## Releasing It All to the Lord

"Lord, confessing terrifies me. Help me to tell You the whole truth and then to tell my story to someone else. Show me who I should talk to. Point me to the person—someone who is trustworthy and safe, who will listen and not condemn. Please give us a safe place and enough time to talk. And, Lord, please take my sins away. Amen."

*Chapter* **11**

# My Sister's Cries

## *Jan's Story*

My name is Jan. It's hard to talk about the horrible things that people do to one another. Personally, I wonder if it isn't harder to stand by helpless in the face of abuse than it is to endure it.

I had just started kindergarten the first time I heard my six-year-old sister, Lisa, scream for help. It was early in the morning and Mommy had just left for work. That's when my older brother, Danny, went into Lisa's bedroom.

I sat at the kitchen table eating a bowl of cereal when I heard Lisa. "No, don't! Stop. Help me. Somebody please help me."

The terror in my sister's voice still echoes in my memory. Horror gripped me. *Why won't Danny help her?*

Ever since our father ran off, we all looked to Danny as "the man of the house." He was nearly a teenager, and Mother trusted him to take care of us. So, I felt confused by Lisa's cries.

I ran to my bedroom, crouched in the corner, and pressed my hands over my ears. It didn't stop the sounds of her screams which stripped every feeling of safety away from my young heart.

Then, the unthinkable occurred to me. *My big brother is the one hurting her. What's he doing? Why is he hurting her?*

His going into her bedroom, her screaming, and me crouching in the corner became routine, but it never became a habit I got used to.

Some mornings, Lisa and I played together before going to school like little girls are supposed to do. I don't really remember those times very clearly. My nights are still filled with the sound of her calling out for help and the feeling of helplessness as I did nothing.

As we grew older, Lisa began to confide the details of the times behind the locked bedroom door. I know it was locked because once, I guess I was about seven, I decided to make him stop hurting her. But when I turned the door handle, it didn't open. Utter despair swept over me. I sunk to the floor and wept.

He terrorized us both in other ways too. His explosive temper often led to verbal, emotional, and physical violence.

Once, when Lisa and I played dolls in her room, Danny came in with a gun. He sat cross-legged on the floor and pointed the gun at us.

"Don't move. If either of you moves, even an inch, I'll shoot the other one."

Back then, I never even considered if the gun was loaded or not. Practically paralyzed by terror, I took shallow breaths so my chest wouldn't heave and hoped with all my might that he wouldn't count the urine running down my leg as movement.

Lisa warned me not to tell about his visits to her bedroom. "If anyone finds out, they'll send me far away to where the bad girls go. We'd never see each other again."

I clung to her.

"Besides," she said, "if I go away, Danny said he'd have to do it to you."

I know now that she really did protect me from him, but in a warped sort of way the guilt of that has covered my life. I hate that I was such a coward—that I wanted so much to be spared that I never did one single thing to help my own sister.

As time passed, she stopped screaming. "I just bite the back of my hand until he's done," she told me. "And I try to think about other things."

I used to try to figure out why Danny did the things he did. Maybe it was because he was forced to look after us since Mom worked. That meant he wasn't free to do all the typical teen stuff.

Or maybe something inside of him snapped when Dad ran off with Danny's piano teacher. Danny never played again, and Dad simply disappeared out of our home and out of our lives. Who knows? I stopped trying to explain things and just focused on hating him.

At the age of fourteen, I snuck out my bedroom window to meet up with nineteen-year-old Jeremy. He raped me that night. I didn't scream, and when I crawled back into my bed, I didn't cry. *I deserve it. I'm so weak. I'm nothing but a coward, too helpless to keep my brother from raping my sister and too weak to stop men from raping me.*

Within two years of that night, I decided that since it was going to happen anyway, I might as well get paid for it. When I climbed out my window that time, I didn't return.

My Pimp, Bongo, treated me real good at first. Since I was young, I brought in a lot of money. Then, he began to give me drugs to "cheer me up." That noose tightened quickly, and soon I did whatever was required to ensure my next fix.

Five years after running away, I showed up unannounced at my mom's house on Thanksgiving. She hugged me when she saw me and told me how good it was to see me, even though I knew I looked like crap.

The whole day she kept saying, "I thought you were dead. I can't believe you're still alive."

I didn't even greet Danny who sat on the couch drinking a can of beer.

Lisa looked good. She had a real job as a receptionist, a girlfriend named Sharon, and a little boy named Zack. That little guy made me smile. When Lisa and I had a few moments alone in the kitchen, I filled her in briefly on my life.

Then, I grabbed her hands. "Listen, I am so, so sorry about what Danny did to you and that I couldn't help."

Tears came, but I didn't let go of her to wipe them away. "I think about it all the time."

Her face paled. "Shush," she said. "He might hear you."

I let go of her hands. "What?"

She motioned to the living room with her head and whispered. "He might be listening."

I swallowed, lowered my voice, and asked, "Does he still— You've moved out. He isn't still?"

"Not since Zack. That's when I told him no more."

"Zack?" Slowly the truth dawned. "Zack is—his?"

She nodded. "Of course. You think I'd ever let another man touch me after all he did?"

*Zach is my brother's—child? How can she be a good mother to a child of his?* All I could manage was a whisper. "Your suffering will never end."

"Sharon is good to Zack." She paused and shrugged. "And she's good to me."

My knees felt wobbly. I rushed to the back door and outside. *Why did I come back? My family is nothing but a trash heap!*

I paced the length of the backyard and tried to calm down. *I need a fix.* I had just decided to leave without eating pumpkin pie, when I saw my brother standing at the back door watching me.

"You still doing tricks to support your habit?"

"Shut up." I spit on the ground.

He lunged at me and squeezed my throat. "No one talks to me that way."

I felt the darkness closing in but aimed my kick perfectly to secure my release. He swore in pain.

Coughing and sputtering I stumbled away. Before running to my car I looked back. Danny was doubled over, moaning.

I managed a raspy curse. "I wish I could hurt you forever for all the pain you've caused us! You're a good-for-nothing loser and a lame excuse for a man."

As I sped away, I vowed to never return. It's been nearly ten years. My hate is as raw as it was then, only stronger. Sometimes it feels like a ball of fire raging in my gut. I'm not getting any younger, and I wonder how much longer I can keep selling my body. And every time I open my legs for another John to get his fix, I hear my sister's cries.

## Relating to the Story

* ❖ How much has Jan's life been influenced by her childhood experiences?

Not at all----------------------A little-------------------Completely

* ❖ In what ways might the pain inflicted on another person impact us?

* ❖ If you were to identify Jan's core issue with her family, what would it be?

* ❖ Do you think it's easier to deal with personal hurts or those inflicted on someone you love?

## Recognizing the Issues ~ Forgiveness Factor

My dearest reader, you have survived abuse, and if you have read to this point, I feel like I know something about you. You are courageous in pursuing healing. Have you followed the suggestions so far? Have you admitted your pain, connected it to your past, rejected the blame, and told your story? If so, I wish I could reach through these pages to give you a quick hug and a big smile.

Now, you are ready to face the biggest hurdle of all. Let me warn you that even the mention of the word may cause you to want to shut this book, or burn it, or erase it from your eReader. But you have grown stronger, and you are ready to face the truth that final freedom only comes through forgiveness.

✤ What is your initial reaction to the need to forgive?

| I will never forgive | They don't deserve it | It's condoning the abuse |
|---|---|---|

Survivors can get stuck in their healing at this point. You may feel confused. First, I'm telling you to place the blame for your abuse squarely on the shoulders of those who hurt you, and now you feel I'm saying to take the burden of guilt away from them.

That is not accurate. The guilty remain guilty. But forgiveness means that you trust God to judge them. Let Him decide what to do about their sinful actions. He is a just God, and we can fully trust Him to judge sin.

The process of forgiveness is taking all of the painful facts to the Lord and laying them at His feet. It's saying, "Lord, You know all things; please deal with this mess." Doing this sets you free. You don't have to be dominated by thoughts of what they did to you. It no longer has to cause you to have ulcers. You let it go, knowing that God has promised to address it as only He is able to do.

Forgiveness is a central issue in finding healing. When we take the steps of admitting our pain, assigning blame, and sharing our story, we begin to fill up the holes in our soul.

If each soul wound had a name, the deepest would be marked unforgiveness. It isn't a hole dug by our perpetrator—we dig it with our own hands in response to the pain inflicted on us. Unforgiveness ends up being a bottomless pit that drains our life away while never touching the life of our perpetrator.

Do you have this place in your soul? Are you refusing to forgive? Do you feel that clinging to the right to be angry somehow makes you feel better or gives you power over those who harmed you?

Or is it just that you think those who abused you don't deserve your forgiveness? It's said that unforgiveness is like drinking poison and waiting for the other person to die.

I personally found it easier to forgive my perpetrator, because of his own troubled past, then to forgive those who looked the other way and allowed the abuse to happen. For a long time, I thought that such selfishness was unforgivable. Maybe you feel this way, too.

Forgiving others isn't optional. God requires it. As stated below:

**Mark 11:25**
> But when you are praying, first forgive anyone
> you are holding a grudge against, so that your
> Father in heaven will forgive your sins, too.

Earlier, we established the absolute need to allow any suppressed memories to surface. Now we're going to explain why this is true. We remember so we can forgive. The Lord requires us to forgive those who sin against us, just like He forgives us of our sin. We can only do this if we remember the offense, face the pain that memory brings, and then choose to forgive those who caused our suffering.

It makes me think of when Jesus hung on the cross. He looked down at those who had nailed Him there and said, "Father, forgive them, for they don't know what they are doing" (Luke 23:34). He faced the fact that those were the people who had hurt Him. He looked right at them and forgave them. We need to acknowledge the offenses against us in order to move on to forgiveness and healing.

Just as confession is a way of life for followers of Jesus, so is forgiveness. I'm not suggesting that this is easy, and I'm also not attempting to diminish your pain.

For a more in-depth study on the topic, I'd like to suggest the book *Choosing Forgiveness* by Nancy Leigh DeMoss (Chicago: Moody Publishers, 2006). She writes, "We can't talk about forgiveness without acknowledging the reality of pain. If we were never hurt, there would be no need for forgiveness" (35).

Just consider for a moment what it cost God to forgive us. He gave His only Son to suffer and die for our sins so we could be forgiven. Look what forgiveness cost Jesus—His very life. Nothing about forgiveness is easy, but God freely offers us forgiveness. In turn, He expects us, as His children, to forgive others.

What if you feel like you can't find any forgiveness in yourself? Begin by understanding that forgiveness isn't something we feel—it's something we choose to do. It's saying, "Lord, You are the One who grants forgiveness. You tell me to forgive. I want to obey You, but I don't know how."

Try to picture it this way. God is the source of forgiveness that is as vast as an ocean. When we are joined to Him, our lives become small streams that can convey His forgiveness to others. We do not have to possess or produce forgiveness; we just need to permit God's forgiveness to flow out from us.

Choosing forgiveness is removing all the debris that is blocking the flow of God's forgiveness from going out to others.

Abuse, anger, hurt, and rage can be like huge logs that dam up our lives. As time moves on, these blocked places attract more and more rubbish causing our stream to become polluted and bitter.

If we refuse to let hurtful memories pile up, we will soon experience the glory of God's forgiveness flowing into and out of us. He fills us with the fresh water of His forgiveness. We simply allow it to flow out to those who have wronged us.

Remember when we discussed "taking every thought captive to the obedience of Christ" (2 Corinthians 10:5 NASB)? Forgiving is an area where we must put this practice into action. We decide to act on what God says and not on how we feel. How do we actually do this?

When unforgiveness grips us, we need to instantly cry out, "Oh, Lord, please help me to let Your forgiveness flow through me. I don't feel like it, but I will choose to forgive."

Some struggle with the concept of forgiving because they feel the perpetrator doesn't deserve to be forgiven. We are not in the position to make that determination. We must choose to release our desire for revenge. God says that is His job. "I will take revenge; I will pay them back. In due time their feet will slip. Their day of disaster will arrive, and their destiny will overtake them (Deuteronomy 32:35)."

You may never witness this, but God is true to His Word. Trust Him. He will punish the guilty. Our part is to release them to God. We must forgive them as we have been forgiven, leaving them to plead their own case before the Lord who is the eternal Judge.

It may help to think of forgiveness as a scar which indicates a healed wound. It's the final step in the healing process. A scar means there is no more gushing pain or tenderness when we recall the ways we were injured. Pastor John R. Wiuff refers to such scars as gifts. He says that once our wounds have healed and scars have formed, we are given extraordinary sight that enables us to relate to the hurts and pains of others.

Surviving sexual abuse will have an impact. Will it be positive or negative? Each of us will choose which type of influence our story and our lives will have.

Some survivors will never seek healing. They will remain wounded and always believe that they are victims in this life. Others might become bitter, mean, and hateful, passing on a legacy of anger or despair to those nearest to them.

If you're reading this book, it is because you want to be well. You're tired of hurting, and you don't want those who you love to be infected by the pain of your traumatic experience. You refuse to drag them into the pit of your suffering. Choosing to deal with your pain will enable you to respond to those you love from a place of wholeness.

Chances are good that your experience has made you more sensitive to the hurts and fears of other people. You may be a person whom others feel comfortable coming to when they have a need or struggle in life. The fact that you have dealt constructively with your suffering means you have something positive to impart to others.

Healing can flow from us in little ways—in kind words, in being patient, in listening well, and in being understanding. Remember that Jesus promised His life in us would become an overflowing spring. Let's look for ways to reach out to others who are hurting. Mother Teresa said, "In this life we cannot do great things. We can only do small things with great love."

## Requesting God's Help

"Lord, thank You for forgiving my sins. Please help me to forgive those who have sinned against me. Let me start to allow Your forgiveness to flow through me to them.

"Help me to let go of bitterness and resentment. I want to be free. "Please, Lord, I can't do this without Your help. Please enable me to forgive. Amen."

## Reflecting on Scripture

This chapter marks the very last verse in the Bible passage we've been studying. Before we take a look at this verse, I'd like to say a few words and a special prayer for readers who may have experienced sexual abuse at the hands of a father figure.

You may find it very difficult to think about God as your Heavenly Father or yourself as His child. When you read about how Jesus responds to our dear sister, try to remember that He is showing us a picture of how a good and loving father relates to his daughter. You may be overcome with emotions that make you want to back away, but instead, please join me in saying this prayer.

*Lord, please reveal Yourself to me as the good, wise, kind, strong, and loving Heavenly Father that You are. Even the term 'father' scares me. Please take my fear. Those who were supposed to protect me failed me. I was not safe. Please help me to see the father-daughter relationship in a new way, according to Your design. Amen.*

Today we will consider the last recorded words of this wonderful story. For the healed woman this was actually the start of a whole new life.

Her encounter with Jesus changed everything about her and the life she had known. She wasn't sick anymore. Her suffering was over. She was free. Meeting Jesus transformed her life. Read today's verse, printed in bold.

## Mark 5:25-34

[25] A woman in the crowd had suffered for twelve years with constant bleeding.

[26] She had suffered a great deal from many doctors, and over the years she had spent everything she had to pay them, but she had gotten no better. In fact, she had gotten worse.

[27] She had heard about Jesus, so she came up behind him through the crowd and touched his robe.

[28] For she thought to herself, "If I can just touch his robe, I will be healed."

[29] Immediately the bleeding stopped, and she could feel in her body that she had been healed of her terrible condition.

[30] Jesus realized at once that healing power had gone out from him, so he turned around in the crowd and asked, "Who touched my robe?"

[31] His disciples said to him, "Look at this crowd pressing around you. How can you ask, 'Who touched me?'"

[32] But he kept on looking around to see who had done it.

[33] Then the frightened woman, trembling at the realization of what had happened to her, came and fell to her knees in front of him and told him what she had done.

³⁴ **And he said to her, "Daughter, your faith has made you well. Go in peace. Your suffering is over."**

We'll look at this verse in sections.

**And he said to her, "Daughter . . ."**

Let's remember what has just happened. Even though she felt afraid, this beloved woman came forward when Jesus called her. She fell at His feet and told Him the whole truth.

Now, Jesus responds to her. Watch carefully and see the tender love of God displayed as He speaks to this woman who has suffered so much in her life. How does Jesus address our dear sister?

Daughter—He calls her daughter. Although the Greek word translated here as daughter is used twenty-seven times in the New Testament, this is the only time it is used to address or describe an individual. It is also the only recorded incidence of Jesus referring to or calling a woman "daughter." It is a very intimate and tender term. It reflects a relationship, a belonging. In a sense, Jesus is saying, "You are my own, a part of my family. You are my little girl." I picture Jesus reaching down to lift up our precious woman as He says, "Daughter."

In the book of John we read these words, "But to all who believed him and accepted him, he gave the right to become children of God" (John 1:12). I think our courageous sister is an example of a woman who believed and accepted Jesus. She bowed before Him, acknowledging that He was worthy. He responded with a term that showed He welcomed her as a part of His family.

It's interesting that the healing of the bleeding woman is reflected in the story of Jairus. These two accounts run parallel to each other. Jairus is an earthly father who deeply loves his little girl, but she is sick and suffering. He fears she will die without help. He makes the effort to get to Jesus and begs for healing to save his daughter's life.

As Jesus makes His way to the place where Jairus' little girl is deathly ill, He stops to interact with the bleeding woman and Jairus' precious little girl dies. In that moment, Jesus and Jairus are both fathers concerned for their daughters. Jesus cared equally for both the woman and the little girl.

At one level this precious woman represents all of the daughters the Lord dearly loves—each little girl who is suffering, every woman with wounds so severe she cannot face life. He is the Good and True Father who responds when suffering women reach out to Him in faith. He stops everything to call each one to Himself. When we come, even in our fear, and when we bow before Him, He responds to us with this declaration, "Daughter."

He claims us! He is not like some earthly parents who abuse, misuse, neglect, or abandon their children. He takes responsibility for us. He is our champion, our protector, and our provider. With that single word, He announced that our dear woman belonged to Him. When we believe and accept Him, this is also true for us. We belong to Him, and that means we are safe at last.

Have you ever longed to have someone take care of you? Have you wanted to simply rest in the fact that you mattered enough to another person that they would promise to always look out for your best interest and take care of your every need? Jesus will. He wants to do that for you.

Won't you come? His arms are outstretched, and He longs to comfort and protect you. He is not waiting to speak condemnation or judgment on you. He knows the whole truth. He waits for you to come, just like He waited for the healed woman; and when you do, He calls you, "Daughter."

## "Your faith . . ."

After establishing His commitment to her, Jesus affirms her strength. He says for all to hear that it is her faith that has made her well. He praises her for her faith.

Notice that Jesus doesn't chide this precious one for pushing through the crowd when she was considered unclean. No, Jesus looked at what was inside of her heart. He saw that faith motivated her.

When we act in faith, it pleases the Lord.[14] So noticing her amazing faith, He encourages our precious woman. In that simple statement I think He was telling her that He fully understood what it took for her to come to Him.

He knew the voices of doubt she had to overcome. He recognized the effort that was required for her to face and push through such a throng of people. He appreciated her faith and was pleased.

## ". . . has made you well."

In Greek, the original word translated here as *well* is *sozo*. *Sozo* has a much broader significance than being restored to good health. Included in its meaning are *to save, rescue* and *to deliver from judgment.*

Jesus does heal our dear sister physically; her bleeding stops. But He does so much more for her. The word *sozo* also addresses her eternal destiny. Jesus is declaring something eternally significant about this woman and her faith. Take a look at how this same word is translated as *saved* in Titus 3:5.

> He *saved* (sozo) us, not because of the righteous
> things we had done, but because of his mercy.
> He washed away our sins, giving us a new birth
> and new life through the Holy Spirit (emphasis
> added).

*Sozo* refers to a total irrevocable healing of the complete person. Let's not miss the most important part of our dear woman's story. Her faith led her to Jesus and He saved her and healed her. The same is true for us; we're saved by faith alone.

While physical and emotional healing are wonderful, the healing that matters for eternity is to be healed in our spirit. To be saved. Our sister left Jesus that day well in her body, soul and spirit.

### "Go in peace."

If God Himself tells you to "go in peace," it is both a command and a reality. Here we see that Jesus, the Prince of Peace, is extending His peace to our dear sister. He is pronouncing a blessing over her as He gives her the gift of His peace. We hear an echo of these same words in a special blessing created by God to be spoken over His people.

> May the LORD bless you and protect you.
>
> May the LORD smile on you
>
> and be gracious to you.
>
> May the LORD show you his favor
>
> and give you his peace (Numbers 6:24-26).

These verses and others reveal the Lord as the "God of peace." It's His peace and He gives it to us. He made the way for us to have peace with Him when He forgave our sins by the death and resurrection of Jesus. He also provides the way for us to have peace with one another when we forgive others as we've been forgiven.

While holding onto anger, rage, and bitterness feeds anxiety within, granting forgiveness brings lasting peace. We can't create this kind of peace.

It doesn't come from moving far away from those who hurt us, or from padding our lives with lots of beautiful things. This peace belongs to God, and He offers it to us as a gift. It is the peace Jesus gave our precious woman as He released her into a new future.

Listen to Jesus' words in John 14:27: "I am leaving you with a gift—peace of mind and heart. And the peace I give is a gift the world cannot give. So don't be troubled or afraid." This verse shows us that there is a type of peace that this world offers that is very different from the peace God gives. His peace doesn't depend on how others treat us or how they react when we extend forgiveness. It is His gift to each of us who come to Him, and no one can take it away.

**"Your suffering is over."**

These are the last recorded words Jesus speaks to this precious one. Jesus always speaks truth, so imagine Him saying these words as a declaration of an unchangeable fact. "YOUR SUFFERING IS OVER." His statement that stands against all odds.

Our dear woman doesn't leave that day burdened with a load of shame and regret. No, Jesus has taken it all—all her sin, all her pain, all her disappointment, and all her suffering. It's all gone. Isn't that wonderful?

This brave woman may have come to Jesus because she believed He could stop her bleeding, but He did so much more than that.

He restored her self-worth when He stopped what He was doing and called out to her. He took her shame when He listened to her confess the whole truth of her story. He wrapped her in love and acceptance when He called her daughter. He acknowledged her strength and affirmed her value when He publicly commended her for her faith.

Jesus blessed her with peace which meant she could go into the future and leave her past behind. And now, His final statement assures her that her total healing is permanent. She is healed. She is changed. She has a new life, and no one and nothing will ever be able to take that away from her.

## Responding to God's Word

Her story can be your story. The hope, healing, and help that Jesus gave to this woman is available to every person. When you reach out to Jesus in faith, He welcomes you into His family. If you have said "yes" to Jesus your life will change and your healing will begin. I want you to know that there is rejoicing in heaven because of you![15]

## Releasing It All to the Lord

"Lord Jesus, thank You that You speak the blessing of peace over me. Thank You that You point the way to a new and bright future.

"Please direct me as I seek to follow Your plan for my life. Thank You that my complete healing has begun. Please help me to live a life that allows Your forgiveness to flow out. Thank You so much for loving me. I want to love You with all of my heart, all of my soul, all of my mind, and all of my strength. Thank You for a new beginning and that You walk with me every step of the way. Amen."

*Chapter* **12**

Dear Reader,

It wouldn't be fair of me to encourage you to tell your story if I am unwilling to share mine with you. This is the way I remember my experience of being sexually abused. It's all true except for the exact timing of events which are approximate. All names but mine have been changed.

# Don't Make Me Tell!

## *Sue's Story*

As we drove up the steep hill of the long street, my daddy said, "Our new house is all the way up at the end of this cul-de-sac."

"And it has two bathrooms, right?" I asked from the back-seat of our red station wagon.

"That's right," he said.

All five members of my family were excited when my dad got a job transfer to another town. We left our single wide trailer behind to move into a real house. For me it meant leaving third grade midway through and starting a new school, but that didn't matter. I just knew we'd all be happy in our new house.

The next morning, as I ran down the sidewalk toward our bus stop, I passed a girl who had walked out of the house next to ours.

I paused and said, "Hi! My name is Susan. I just moved in next door. I'm in the third grade."

She looked shyly at me with big brown eyes, much like my own. "Hi. I'm Ann, I'm ten, and I'm in the fifth grade."

"Want to play after school?" I asked.

She nodded slowly.

I waved before continuing my run to the bottom of the hill.

That's how our lifelong friendship began. Ann and I spent endless hours over the next four years playing Barbie dolls, listening to records of The Beatles, and pretending. During the long summer days in sunny California, we practically lived in her swimming pool where we had underwater tea parties and played mermaids.

We were always happy when we were together, but Ann's life, when I wasn't there, was filled with abuse at the hands of her stepfather, Tom. One day, about a year after we met, she whispered her secret to me.

"Tom makes me touch his private places, and he touches me, too."

I stared at her. "Really? That's gross."

She chewed her bottom lip. "I know. But it happens all the time."

"You should tell."

"I have—but my mom always makes me say that I'm lying."

"Why?"

"She likes our house and all the nice things."

"Oh." I'd heard all my nine-year-old mind could handle. "Let's swing on the swing set."

"Okay."

After she confided in me, I desperately wanted to do something to help her. Yet, it never occurred to me to tell my parents. In my family we never talked about deep things or feelings.

My parents are good people. My dad worked hard and my mother cooked dinner every night. They took care of my siblings and me, but we were never really involved or emotionally connected to each other.

Our family didn't talk about what was going on inside or what we felt. I can't remember ever being asked about the events of my day or why I seemed sad. It just wasn't what we did in my home.

During that time, we were a foster family for newborn babies. An infant would come, and my mother would take care of the baby for a few months until the little one was placed for adoption and leave. Then, we'd get another newborn. This meant that a social worker named Mrs. Poke, would periodically come to our home.

One day, I asked my mother for an envelope and stamp and Mrs. Poke's address. I was relieved that she didn't ask me why I wanted it and thankful that she gave me what I needed. I wrote a letter telling Mrs. Poke about Ann's abuse. Eventually, that resulted in some intense interviews by school counselors for Ann.

"They don't really believe me," Ann said. "Mr. Bass just wants to hear about the exact things that Tom does to me. He keeps asking me to tell him more and more, and wants all these details. I'm not going back. It's too embarrassing. I told him everything was okay and said I didn't want to talk about it anymore."

Sometime after that, I found myself alone in Ann's house with Tom. I'm not sure how or why this happened.

Tom asked me, "Want to see a movie?"

Those were the days before DVD or even VHS videos. Besides an occasional movie on TV, I only got to see movies at the theater. When I did, it was always a treat. "Yes," I said. "Which one?" I was hoping to see *Bambi* or *The Parent Trap*.

"It's a special one of mine," he said. "Let me get the projector."

"Okay." I felt excited as I waited on the couch in their den.

Tom came back with a small hand crank projector and a spool of film. He turned out the lights. An image projected onto the wall, and as he cranked the handle, it began to move.

"Do you see it?" he asked.

"Yeah. What is it?"

"What does it look like to you?"

I stared at the fuzzy image and thought it looked sort of furry. "A kitty cat?" I guessed.

"No." He slowed down the movie so I could see the movement. Then he said, "This is a close up picture of a man's penis going in and out of a woman's vagina. See right here," he pointed, "this is the man's part. Watch. Watch it go in and out, in and out. This is how a man and woman have sex."

"Oh," I said. My face got hot, and I felt so uncomfortable. I was thankful that the lights were off. I felt disappointed that we didn't see a real movie like *Bambi*. I wasn't at all impressed with Tom's movie. "I've got to go home now," I said.

"Ann, will be back soon. Don't you want to stay and wait for her?"

"No." I left.

Another incident happened on a Saturday when Ann and I were trying to earn money.

Tom told us, "I'll pay you a penny for every weed you pull."

It sounded like an easy way to make money, but after working an hour, we had hardly any weeds in our bucket. We were kneeling in their front yard pulling weeds, when Tom joined us. "Let me help," he said.

He squatted right beside us, his knees wide apart. His jeans had large holes in the crotch, and he wasn't wearing underwear.

Tom did this type of thing often. Like having us swim under his legs in the pool when his suit didn't properly cover him. He also showed me comic books with naked people and talked to me about the drawings.

He pointed. "This lady has really big boobs, doesn't she?"

Other times he would talk to me about how my body would be changing soon and I'd be a woman.

Looking back, I see that Tom was calculating in his abuse as he tried to slowly ease me into accepting his behavior as natural. I didn't like Tom's games, but I took my cues from

Ann. I even asked her opinion when he exposed himself to us. She acted like it was normal and just shrugged at my concerns.

I now know how horribly Tom abused her when they were alone. I imagine the games he invented that included me may have seemed harmless to Ann compared to what he demanded of her privately. But I didn't like it. Still, I really wanted to be with Ann, and her stepfather was part of the package.

One night, in particular, remains seared in my memory. The three of us were in a tent in their backyard. Her stepfather said that the tent needed to be aired out before their family went camping.

He set it up in the day and said we could go inside.

"Wow, it's big enough for your whole family," I said. Everything had a blue tint from the sun coming through the sides of the tent and it smelt musty.

Tom stood at the door and watched as we twirled in circles inside the tent. "Do you girls want to sleep in the tent tonight?"

"Really?" Ann said. She lived a very controlled and sad life and was hardly ever allowed to have sleepovers.

I jumped up and down. "Yes, yes."

"Okay, Susan," Tom said. "If your parents say it's okay."

Ann and I stared at each other as if to say, "It will be a blast to have a sleepover in the tent!"

That's when Tom told us about the one requirement.

"You can sleep in the tent under one condition. I have to come out here and stay with you."

"You're going to stay in the tent with us?" I asked.

"Not the whole night," he said. "Just at first, for a little while. I want to be sure you girls are safe."

Ann and I exchanged glances and shrugged. If that was what was required to have the rest of the night to ourselves, we'd do it.

We were not safe out there in the tent that night. Tom subjected us to perverted games of exposure. In one game, he held a black hat over his genitals and insisted we shout, "Hat's off." When we did, he exposed himself to us.

Next, he forced us to stroke, rub, and touch his penis. I hated this but didn't want Ann to have to do it alone. I kept glancing at her as if to say, "If we do this, will he leave so we can be alone?"

Even though Tom had promised he would only stay for a while, he just wouldn't leave. Finally, after being forced to participate in many of his so-called games, he insisted we get into our nightgowns and turn out the light.

Tom lay between us saying he wanted to give us a thigh rub. He said it would feel good, like a back rub. After that, he said he would leave.

Tom began stroking, touching, and rubbing me. He quickly moved from my legs to between my legs. To say I felt uncomfortable with his grown-up hand exploring my body is an understatement. I kept asking Ann if she liked what he was doing. She assured me that it was fine. I couldn't see her and didn't realize that he wasn't touching her the same way he touched me.

Tom kept fondling me. As he did, a sour taste rose in my mouth. I wanted out of there. I wanted him to stop. I didn't like it. But I also wanted to spend the night with Ann in the tent. I tried so hard to endure, to appease Tom so that he would leave and allow Ann and I to enjoy our sleepover. His inappropriate, abusive touching went on a long time—way too long.

Looking back, I realize that I simply couldn't handle the conflict caused by having my young body sexually aroused, long before the appropriate time and in a perverted manner. I literally felt ill and thought I might vomit. So, just when my body started to respond, I jumped up and ran out of the tent. Ann followed me to be sure I was okay.

When we returned to the tent, Ann's stepfather had gone. For as clear as my recollection of those perverted events are, I have no memory of the rest of the night. I don't know if Ann and I stayed out there in the tent, if we went to sleep in her bedroom, or if I went home.

Not long afterwards, the details of our night in the tent came to light unexpectedly because of an obscene photograph that Ann's mother found.

When she confronted Ann and showed her the picture, Ann again told her mother that Tom was sexually abusing her.

When her mother accused her of lying, Ann said, "Ask Susan. He's done things to her, too." Then she told her mother the details of our night in the tent.

In response, Ann's mother said, "If this is true, go and get Susan. Tell her to come here—right now. I want to talk to her."

When Ann showed up at my door, I could tell she'd been crying.

"You have to come right now," she said. "My mom wants to talk to you about the night in the tent."

Horror seized me and shame covered me. I felt guilty and sure didn't want to have to talk about that horrible night. By the time we walked into Ann's house, I was already near tears.

Fear and embarrassment went with me into the small den where the curtains were never opened. Ann's mother spent most of her time in this room, watching soap operas on TV while she drank canned beer and smoked cigarettes.

Ann's mother sat in her usual place as I stumbled into the dark, smoke-filled room. Unable to look her in the eyes, I stared at her crossed legs and watched her top foot bounce rapidly. She puffed urgently on a cigarette in her right hand. Her long manicured nails were painted a deep red.

She pointed to the sofa. "Sit."

I hung my head as Ann's mother began to interrogate me about the night in the tent. In between sobs I told her about

Tom's games and the way he made us touch him. I did not describe the way he fondled me and made me feel defiled and violated. I only said that I thought I might throw up and that I ran out of the tent.

Ann sat in silence on the large recliner across from me. My clearest impression of the whole ordeal is a suffocating sense of shame. I knew that what went on that night in the tent was very wrong—and somehow I felt a crushing weight of guilt because it had happened to me.

As I sat sobbing on their sofa, Ann's mother called her husband on the phone. She yelled at him. "How stupid can you be?" She shouted for a long time about his carelessness and said something like, "She's a neighbor girl. You could go to jail."

The meaning of these statements didn't register with me. I was too overcome with shame to think about anything else. After she hung up, Ann's mother sat next to me on the sofa.

In an accusing tone she said, "If this is all true, go home and tell your mother. Right now. Go home and tell her everything!"

The thought horrified me. "No," I cried. Nothing I had experienced up to that point compared with the fear that gripped me when Ann's mother insisted that I tell my parents about what had happened. "No, I can't. Please, don't make me."

In writing this account, I've asked myself why I didn't tell. In facing the reasons, I have discovered another wound that I have denied for all these years. It's the wound caused by not feeling close enough to my parents to automatically go to them with my problems. Why didn't I see them as my protectors, as the ones I could trust with every detail of my life?

From my earliest memory, I have felt loved by God. His love has always wrapped around me like a soft blanket on a cold day. As a young child, I remember praying in the night when I felt afraid. His presence has always been my constant comfort and makes me know that I am special to Him.

I can't explain why this is true. Perhaps, it's because of the nuns who worked at the hospital and took care of me as a premature baby who weighed less than three pounds. I've imagined them praying for me. I'm grateful for this deep assurance of God's love.

While I have never doubted that my parents also loved me, I didn't feel emotionally connected enough to go to them when I was abused.

I consider my upbringing to be typical for a two parent, middle-class American family. My parents are good people and did the best they could in raising us.

They were never cruel, neglectful, or abusive. I'm so grateful to them that my practical needs were always met; we had a home, food, clothes, and a car. I went to school, a community dance class, and even an orthodontist.

My father went to work to provide for us and my mother cooked dinner every night. She sewed clothes for my Barbie doll and costumes for Ann and I. Even though I don't remember hugs, kisses, tender touches, songs, or story reading, or that my mother ever told me she loved me when I was young, I never doubted that she did.

Yet, we never talked about what was on my mind or in my heart. I do not remember one time when I confided my deepest feelings to either of my parents. We had very little emotional connection. I know that my parents didn't intentionally wound me or fail to protect me, but it happened.

Our lack of emotional connection is partly to blame for my abuse. In a different environment I would have known that telling my parents is the very first thing to do when a neighbor showed me a pornographic movie. But in my home, we didn't talk about anything personal. When I didn't tell, I was just following the rules I'd learned.

## *Recognizing the Issues ~ Speak Up*

I regret that I didn't stand up to Ann's mother and say, "I will tell. I'll tell my parents the truth about Tom and about what he did. And I'll tell them that you always force Ann to say she's lying." I had the power to break the cycle of abuse by speaking out. But I didn't.

Each of us can break the power of our abuse by speaking out. It may have happened years ago. You may have carefully guarded it as a secret, but until you speak the truth about your experience, you will never be free. In her booklet, printed by IVP Books, *Healing from Sexual Abuse*, Kathleen writes, "In order to put shame to rest, the victim must tell her story to someone who can help her" (17).

I'm ashamed that I refused to tell. I should have told. In that moment, there was the possibility that what I said could have changed things for my friend. But I kept silent. My own fear, my own shame, kept me from speaking up and from telling the truth. Not anymore! It's been many years, but now I am speaking up and speaking out for those who have survived abuse.

It occurs to me that my sexual abuse may be very mild compared to what you endured. But as author Cecil Murphey says, "It's the worst story I know, because it's my story."

My experience had very negative effects on my ability to enjoy intimacy in my marriage. The fact that sexual abuse, even as limited as what I experienced, could cause such severe problems convinced me of the need for healing for all survivors, regardless of the details of our individual encounters.

Ann's stepfather never touched me again after his perversions in the tent were exposed. But it didn't stop him from molesting Ann until she was old enough to move out of the house. My father got a job transfer some time later and we moved to another town several hours away.

Even as a young girl, I knew that what had happened to me wasn't right. I also believed that God is good and that He's the One who created male and female and sex (at least as a way to have babies). So, at a young age, I determined to try to understand God's design for human sexuality.

I am not an expert on sexuality or on sexual abuse. I don't have a degree, and I'm not a professional anything. But I do have the experience of being young and innocent and having an adult prey on my childlike trust for his own selfish reasons.

As I grew older, I began to seek a biblical view of sexuality and to understand as much as I could about God's good design for sex. Over the years, this has led me to speak on related topics, to write articles and stories, and now, to write this book.

Once married, I struggled with flashbacks. My body would shut down, just as it had when I was a child, at that same point of arousal. These invasions into the intimate times I shared with my husband made sexual enjoyment impossible for me. This caused guilt and deep disappointment. I knew I needed to be healed from my childhood trauma.

The fact that my experience wasn't as horrific as Ann's didn't diminish my need for healing. If you have ever thought that your experience isn't bad enough for you to seek healing, think again. You were violated and that has its negative effects. Admit your pain and face it. Find healing.

Maybe your abuser even told you, like mine did, that you were just "playing a game." Maybe he said that it was no big deal. But any sexual conduct between an adult and child is a big deal that steals innocence and has ongoing negative consequences. Do not diminish or dismiss your experience.

Only you can determine how the betrayal hurt you, and only you can decide to find healing.

The fact that Tom's selfish acts could rob me and my husband of something so special seemed totally unfair and unacceptable! God intended for sex to be a good and joyful part of my marriage, and since that was His plan, I decided to do whatever I needed to get well. I'm so glad I didn't settle for less and very thankful for a patient husband and for the Lord who has healed and is healing my wounded heart.

Every survivor who has helped with this book has found the courage to talk about her experience. Each will confirm that telling someone is essential to healing. It's sort of like feeling nauseous and then feeling so much better after you throw up. For some reason, keeping all that evil hidden away inside is very unhealthy. I think it has to do with the fact that God is light. Look at what Jesus says about this in John 3:20: "All who do evil hate the light and refuse to go near it for fear their sins will be exposed."

When we bring what is dark out into the light, it is exposed and it can't survive. Light consumes the darkness, but darkness can't consume the light. It only takes a tiny flame to spread light in a dark place.

Once, when on a tour of Carlsbad Caverns, our guide told us to stop walking. Then, he turned off his flashlight. The darkness was thick enough to feel. Our guide then lit a match, and that tiny bit of light transformed the whole area. Bringing our story out of our memory bank into the here and now is sort of like that. The simple act of speaking, or writing, the truth will transform your experience from something that controls you into something that you can control.

This book is my way of bringing the dark things that happened to me into the light. I am finally brave enough to tell the truth about what happened by putting it in print for anyone to read. During the writing process, the Lord reminded me that even as a young girl I used writing when I wrote that letter to try to help my friend who was being sexually abused. Now, it is years later and I am still writing, still longing to help.

The Lord gave me a story that illustrates my passion to see survivors find healing in Jesus. As I recorded this little story, it seemed so vivid and real to me that it has infused every moment of my past and future with purpose. It rises over my life like a silent proclamation.

> *I rush into a dark forest where a little girl stands shivering. Her innocence has been stolen and my heart breaks. Scooping her up, I hold her and soothe her. "You're safe now, Little One. Your suffering is over."*

> *She smiles at me and we walk hand-in-hand out of the woods into a large field, tall with ripe wheat. The wheat parts in front of us as we move forward.*

> *When I next look at this child beside me, she is a grown woman. We have to stop because she cannot go on. Looking over my shoulder, I see that a heavy, rusty chain is holding her back, binding her to that painful place from where she has come. She sees the shackles too, and begins to tremble and sob. I want to help her. I want her to be free to go on joyfully into her future. So I place a large empty canvas between her and her past.*

> *The woman begins painting her pain—every single detail of her abuse. She uses angry colors and sharp contrasts. Her body heaves as she wildly splashes the insults, shame, humiliation, and betrayal onto the waiting canvas.*

*It is hard work, but she keeps at it. She goes on and on and on until there is no white space left—only a mass of confusion, pain, and shame.*

*The intensity of the exertion causes her to tremble and sweat until at last, she is exhausted. I watch but do not attempt to help. I know this is her story and she must tell it.*

*When she finishes the final brush stroke, she hands the painting to me. I pour the colors into the cup of my own abuse, swirling the events into a mass of thick concentrated liquid that I spill out upon the ground and cover with fresh soil.*

*From that mound of soil, green stems start to spout and soon soft colored flowers grow. I've never seen such beautiful blooms or known such sweet scents! As I watch, a large hand gathers all the wonderful fragrant flowers and places them in my arms.*

*I begin to dance with the bouquet while tossing the petals into the wind that swirls above the heads of countless sobbing women who have replaced the grain fields surrounding me.*

*The petals hold healing power. As the petals land softly on their heads, the women begin to tell their own stories. They cry as they share their sorrows. Their tears splash on the ground where they stand, and from the moist soil, flowers sprout and bloom.*

*One-by-one, each woman gathers her own flowers and skips off to another place to scatter her own petals in the wind. My heart swells with the joy of sharing the beauty of the flowers with them. I lift my voice to my precious Lord who has healed my broken heart.*

"As You give me opportunity, Lord, I will tell my story. I'll speak of the pain and of the healing. Allow me to be involved in rescuing others who are still wounded. Oh, Lord, let me be an instrument of healing. Bind up each broken heart, and please, please, Lord, bring beauty out of the ashes of our abuse. Amen."

# Final Note

My Dear Reader,

The time we've shared in the pages of this book is ending. For me personally it's a great accomplishment, since I often start projects with a lot of enthusiasm but just as often fail to finish what I begin.

On the other hand, it seems sad to say good-bye to you. I have had you in my heart, on my mind, and in my prayers for nearly two years. I've pictured you as I've worked, longing to take you by the hand and lead you a step closer to Jesus.

This is my desire. I hope with all my heart that I have accomplished this, for He is the One who made you and understands you. He's crazy about you and has great surprises and joy awaiting you. He flung the galaxies into existence yet numbers each hair on your head. He knows each word you'll say before you speak it. His tender love is strong enough to support you as you work your way toward healing.

I'm praying you will let go of your struggle and find your rest in His waiting arms. He alone is our safe place. In Him all of our questions are answered, and all of our hopes are realized.

I extend my love to you in the name of Jesus. Now that you have begun the journey to healing, I pray you will continue until, like our dear woman, you hear the words of Jesus, "Daughter, your faith has made you well. Go in peace. Your suffering is over."

Because of His love,

Sue Cameron

# *Appendix*

## BIBLE READINGS TO GO ALONG WITH CHAPTER 8.

### Psalm 55

[1] Listen to my prayer, O God. Do not ignore my cry for help!

[2] Please listen and answer me, for I am over-whelmed by my troubles.

[3] My enemies shout at me, making loud and wicked threats. They bring trouble on me and angrily hunt me down.

[4] My heart pounds in my chest. The terror of death assaults me.

[5] Fear and trembling overwhelm me, and I can't stop shaking.

[6] Oh, that I had wings like a dove; then I would fly away and rest!

[7] I would fly far away to the quiet of the wilderness.

[8] How quickly I would escape—far from this wild storm of hatred.

[9] Confuse them, Lord, and frustrate their plans, for I see violence and conflict in the city.

[10] Its walls are patrolled day and night against invaders, but the real danger is wickedness within the city.

[11] Everything is falling apart; threats and cheating are rampant in the streets.

[12] It is not an enemy who taunts me—I could bear that. It is not my foes who so arrogantly insult me—I could have hidden from them.

¹³ Instead, it is you—my equal, my companion and close friend.

¹⁴ What good fellowship we once enjoyed as we walked together to the house of God.

¹⁵ Let death stalk my enemies; let the grave swallow them alive, for evil makes its home within them.

¹⁶ But I will call on God, and the LORD will rescue me.

¹⁷ Morning, noon, and night I cry out in my distress, and the LORD hears my voice.

¹⁸ He ransoms me and keeps me safe from the battle waged against me, though many still oppose me.

¹⁹ God, who has ruled forever, will hear me and humble them. For my enemies refuse to change their ways; they do not fear God.

²⁰ As for my companion, he betrayed his friends; he broke his promises.

²¹ His words are as smooth as butter, but in his heart is war. His words are as soothing as lotion, but underneath are daggers!

²² Give your burdens to the LORD, and he will take care of you. He will not permit the godly to slip and fall.

²³ But you, O God, will send the wicked down to the pit of destruction. Murderers and liars will die young, but I am trusting you to save me.

## Lamentations 3

¹ I am the one who has seen the afflictions that come from the rod of the LORD's anger.

² He has led me into darkness, shutting out all light.

³ He has turned his hand against me again and again, all day long.

⁴ He has made my skin and flesh grow old. He has broken my bones.

⁵ He has besieged and surrounded me with anguish and distress.

⁶ He has buried me in a dark place, like those long dead.

⁷ He has walled me in, and I cannot escape. He has bound me in heavy chains.

⁸ And though I cry and shout, he has shut out my prayers.

⁹ He has blocked my way with a high stone wall; he has made my road crooked.

¹⁰ He has hidden like a bear or a lion, waiting to attack me.

¹¹ He has dragged me off the path and torn me in pieces, leaving me helpless and devastated.

¹² He has drawn his bow and made me the target for his arrows.

¹³ He shot his arrows deep into my heart.

¹⁴ My own people laugh at me. All day long they sing their mocking songs.

¹⁵ He has filled me with bitterness and given me a bitter cup of sorrow to drink.

¹⁶ He has made me chew on gravel. He has rolled me in the dust.

¹⁷ Peace has been stripped away, and I have forgotten what prosperity is.

¹⁸ I cry out, "My splendor is gone! Everything I had hoped for from the LORD is lost!"

¹⁹ The thought of my suffering and homelessness is bitter beyond words.

²⁰ I will never forget this awful time, as I grieve over my loss.

²¹ Yet I still dare to hope when I remember this:

²² The faithful love of the LORD never ends! His mercies never cease.

²³ Great is his faithfulness; his mercies begin afresh each morning.

²⁴ I say to myself, "The LORD is my inheritance; therefore, I will hope in him!"

²⁵ The LORD is good to those who depend on him, to those who search for him.

²⁶ So it is good to wait quietly for salvation from the LORD.

²⁷ And it is good for people to submit at an early age to the yoke of his discipline:

²⁸ Let them sit alone in silence beneath the LORD's demands.

²⁹ Let them lie face down in the dust, for there may be hope at last.

³⁰Let them turn the other cheek to those who strike them and accept the insults of their enemies.

³¹ For no one is abandoned by the Lord forever.

³² Though he brings grief, he also shows compassion because of the greatness of his unfailing love.

³³ For he does not enjoy hurting people or causing them sorrow.

³⁴ If people crush underfoot all the prisoners of the land,

<sup>35</sup> if they deprive others of their rights in defiance of the Most High,

<sup>36</sup> if they twist justice in the courts—doesn't the Lord see all these things?

<sup>37</sup> Who can command things to happen without the Lord's permission?

<sup>38</sup> Does not the Most High send both calamity and good?

<sup>39</sup> Then why should we, mere humans, complain when we are punished for our sins?

<sup>40</sup> Instead, let us test and examine our ways. Let us turn back to the LORD.

<sup>41</sup> Let us lift our hearts and hands to God in heaven and say,

<sup>42</sup> "We have sinned and rebelled, and you have not forgiven us.

<sup>43</sup> "You have engulfed us with your anger, chased us down, and slaughtered us without mercy.

<sup>44</sup> You have hidden yourself in a cloud so our prayers cannot reach you.

<sup>45</sup> You have discarded us as refuse and garbage among the nations.

<sup>46</sup> "All our enemies have spoken out against us.

<sup>47</sup> We are filled with fear, for we are trapped, devastated, and ruined."

<sup>48</sup> Tears stream from my eyes because of the destruction of my people!

<sup>49</sup> My tears flow endlessly; they will not stop

<sup>50</sup> until the LORD looks down from heaven and sees.

<sup>51</sup> My heart is breaking over the fate of all the women of Jerusalem.

<sup>52</sup> My enemies, whom I have never harmed, hunted me down like a bird.

**53** They threw me into a pit and dropped stones on me.

**54** The water rose over my head, and I cried out, "This is the end!"

**55** But I called on your name, LORD, from deep within the pit.

**56** You heard me when I cried, "Listen to my pleading! Hear my cry for help!"

**57** Yes, you came when I called; you told me, "Do not fear."

**58** Lord, you are my lawyer! Plead my case! For you have redeemed my life.

**59** You have seen the wrong they have done to me, LORD. Be my judge, and prove me right.

**60** You have seen the vengeful plots my enemies have laid against me.

**61** LORD, you have heard the vile names they call me. You know all about the plans they have made.

**62** My enemies whisper and mutter as they plot against me all day long.

**63** Look at them! Whether they sit or stand, I am the object of their mocking songs.

**64** Pay them back, LORD, for all the evil they have done.

**65** Give them hard and stubborn hearts, and then let your curse fall on them!

**66** Chase them down in your anger, destroying them beneath the LORD's heavens.

# Endnotes

[1] http://www.allaboutcounseling.com/sexual_abuse.htm#sa7. "It's believed that 1 in 3 girls is sexually abused, and a general consensus of 1 in 5 to 1 in 7 boys is sexually abused."

[2] All clinicians seeing pediatric patients for vaginal bleeding should have sexual abuse near the top of the differential diagnosis list. *Abnormal vaginal bleeding in the nonpregnant patient.* R.V. Daniels, C. McCuskey / Emerg Med Clin N Am 21 (2003) 751–772, 755.

[3] Fred and Florence Littauer. *Freeing Your Mind from Memories that Bind* (San Bernardino, CA: Here's Life Publishers, 1988), 55.

[4] Littauer, 172.

[5] For similar verses read: Mark 9:42 and Luke 17:2.

[6] "If a woman has a flow of blood for many days that is unrelated to her menstrual period, or if the blood continues beyond the normal period, she is ceremonially unclean. As during her menstrual period, the woman will be unclean as long as the discharge continues" (Leviticus 15:25).

[7] G. Campbell Morgan, G. Campbell, *The Gospel According to Luke* (Old Tappan, NJ: Fleming H. Revell Co., 1931), 115.

[8] http://en.wikipedia.org/wiki/Misconceptions_about_HIV_and_AIDS

[9] "The thief's purpose is to steal and kill and destroy. My purpose is to give them a rich and satisfying life" (John 10:10).

[10] "You know my thoughts even when I'm far away. You know what I am going to say even before I say it, LORD" (Psalm 139:2, 4).

[11] The NAS New Testament Hat Greek Lexicon, Strong's Number: 5273. An actor, stage player, a dissembler (to disguise or conceal one's true motives, feelings, or beliefs) pretender, hypocrite.

12 "You say, 'I am allowed to do anything'—but not everything is good for you. You say, 'I am allowed to do anything'—but not everything is beneficial" (1 Corinthians 10:23).

13 "The next day John saw Jesus coming toward him and said, 'Look! The Lamb of God who takes away the sin of the world!'" (John 1:29).

14 "It is impossible to please God without faith. Anyone who wants to come to him must believe that God exists and that he rewards those who sincerely seek him" (Hebrews 11:6).

15 "I tell you that in the same way there will be more rejoicing in heaven over one sinner who repents than over ninety-nine righteous persons who do not need to repent " (Luke 15:7 NIV).

ORDERING INFORMATION
Order additional copies at:


www.GrammySue.com


Quantity discounts are available.

## Hope, Healing, and Help
### for Survivors of Sexual Abuse
#### A Faith-based Journey to Healing


Sue Cameron is an inspirational speaker and Bible teacher who creatively conveys God's grace and truth. She brings fresh insight to topics related to being a godly woman, such as: "Loving Your Husband," "Healing from Hurts," and "Developing a Listening Heart."


*"I'd love to fashion a presentation based on your vision, needs, or Bible passage."*